M000209136

No Dream Deferred

Withdrawn from library collection
Second hand sale authorized by
Arapahoe Library District

No Dream Deferred

WHY BLACK AND LATINO FAMILIES ARE CHOOSING HOMESCHOOL

• • •

Zakkiyya Chase

3 1393 01833 9137

© 2016 Zakkiyya Chase
All rights reserved.

ISBN: 0997893419
ISBN 13: 9780997893410
Library of Congress Control Number: 2016913344
Empowered Home Educators, Jonesboro, GA

Dedication

I would like to dedicate this book to my son Arcani, my mother Jacqueline, and my father Hafez. Thank you all for teaching me to be the greatest version of myself, to always follow my passions, and to take pride in my intellect. My pen is my sword and I am ready for battle.

Introduction

● ● ●

THERE'S SOMETHING IN THE AIR. A sweet-smelling, nostalgia-inducing scent. The scent enters the nose, fills the body with delight, and then escapes through the mouth by laughter. It is the scent of hope. The scent of promise. The scent of dreams yet to be realized.

Call it whatever you like, but it's certainly in the air, and black and Latino families across the nation are covered in it. It lingers in their clothes, fills their homes, coats their meals, echoes in their music, and follows them around town. The scent is as unique as it is unmistakable, yet some dare call it a stench. A foul residue of a culture doomed to fail.

Why else would the black and Hispanic bodies possessing such a smell be subject to immense ridicule, isolation, and prejudice? Certainly something must be wrong with a group of people if they are found everywhere yet seemingly belong nowhere.

They are not happily welcomed into the good neighborhoods, good hospitals, or good schools. They are not given the same job opportunities, business loans, or scholarships. Even as children they are too old for tenderness, too foreign for compassion, and too wicked for innocence. What is to become of a community that views itself as brilliant yet the outside world sees as a nuisance? Are we to tell new parents that their babies are somehow tainted, broken, and in need of repair? What are these parents to do in order to secure better life chances for their children? Since education is viewed as the gateway to success, education has become a life-or-death pursuit for families of color. In the black and Latino communities, children who remain uneducated are automatically sentenced to death. This could be death by poverty, death by incarceration, or death by violence.

Families of color have tried many solutions to properly educate their children—integrated public schools, expensive private schools, and alternative charter schools. All of these "well-meaning" options have yielded poor results in their own respects. Children of color have faced inequality, discrimination, unjust suspensions, special education/ADHD labels, denied entrance into gifted programs, physical and emotional abuse, alienation, and even arrest in institutions that were created for education and upward mobility. These sobering facts have left many parents feeling hopeless and incapable of helping their children.

However, in recent years, a newly discovered alternative has gained attention—homeschooling. Homeschooling has been in existence for years and has been viewed nationally as a popular option for Christian, conservative white Americans who object to the separation of religion in government and public education. Within the past two decades, homeschooling has gained a new resurgence from an unlikely demographic. The newest members of the homeschool community are black and Latino families, whose motivations for homeschooling their children go beyond mere ideological reasons and have become a method of creating equality in an educational system that has abandoned the goals of school integration and has instead fallen into a new era of apartheid education.

How the Book Is Organized

● ● ●

IN THIS BOOK, I WILL take you on a journey through the evolution of the black and Latino education in America, address the chronic issues faced by people of color in brick-and-mortar schools, share evidence of rampant discrimination and de facto segregation in the American education system, share personal stories from black and Latino families who currently homeschool their kids, and shed light on the benefits of homeschooling children of all ages.

In part 1, our focus will be on the history of the black American struggle for the right to learn and to be educated in public schools. We will examine the methods utilized by both freedmen and slaves to learn and teach each other. We will look at the free schools created by white missionaries as an act of civil service and also review efforts made by black teachers during segregation to educate their students and boost morale. Two stories by black families currently homeschooling follow this section.

In part 2, we will discuss the Latino experience in America, the failings of American schools to support the Latino community, and the education crisis that has persisted for Latino students in terms of securing an education while living in impoverished areas, having their language treated as a nuisance, and having the value of their heritage ignored. A story by a Latina homeschooling mother closes out this section.

In part 3, we will talk about the class of 1980. The class of 1980 was the first class in American history to have spent its entire K–12 education (years 1967–1980) in fully integrated schools. The white and minority students attended school together under federally mandated desegregation efforts. Children were bused out to surrounding districts, reassigned to new districts, or were part of an influx of minority students into a formerly all-white area. Their lives after graduation provide an astonishing contrast to the fond experiences they had while in desegregated public school and beg the question of whether or not federal desegregation was actually successful.

In part 4, we dive into the hidden world of the public and private school education experience for children of color. We will discuss the aspirations and failures of the public school system as well as the implicit biases within the private school setting. We will also examine the zero-tolerance disciplinary policies being aggressively used in popular charter schools and the greater implications these policies have for the black and Latino communities. Homeschool family stories are included here as well.

Lastly, part 5 relates the growing homeschool movement among parents of color. Homeschooling provides a unique opportunity for self-healing and self-determination for families of color. We will delve into the benefits of homeschooling for both the student and family and present it as a tangible solution for parents of color seeking to give their children an alternative to the failing educational system. We will end this section with a Q&A of common homeschool questions and concerns.

It is my goal as an author that this book provides a well-rounded view of the true reasons why black and Latino families are seeking to homeschool their kids and to inspire curious families to take the plunge and embrace homeschooling as a means of restoring inquisitiveness, tenderness, and excitement into their children's education.

Part 1: The Origins of Black Education in America

• • •

Hey Black Child

Do you know who you are

Who you really are

Do you know you can be what you want to be if you try to be what you can be

Hey Black Child

Do you know where you are going

Where you're really going

Do you know you can learn what you want to learn if you try to learn what you can learn

Hey Black Child

Do you know you are strong

I mean really strong

Do you know you can do what you want to do if you try to do what you can do

Hey Black Child

Be what you can be

Learn what you must learn

Do what you can do

And tomorrow your nation

Will be what you want it to be

—"Hey, Black Child," by Countee Cullen

Self-Taught and Ready to Run: The Double Lives of Black American Slaves

● ● ●

Slaves were not allowed books, pen, ink, nor paper, to improve their
minds. But it seems to me now, that I was particularly observing
and apt to retain what came under my observation...all that I heard
about liberty and freedom to slaves, I never forgot. Among other
good trades, I learned the art of running away to perfection.

—HENRY BIBB, FORMER SLAVE AND FOUNDER
OF THE VOICE OF THE FUGITIVE

THE THOUGHT OF A SLAVE in America at best conjures up images of vast cotton or tobacco fields, black people barefoot in tattered clothes, faces captured in photographs devoid of emotion with eyes staring blankly ahead. At worst, we think of slaves as human property subject to brutal violence, exploitation, or death at any moment. However, it is rare that we think of slaves as masters of disguise. Those same blank faces captured in photographs were also the faces of people quietly conspiring to liberate themselves. The first step in liberation most often began by obtaining literacy. The ability to read was worth more than gold. The capacity to read and understand meant the ability to learn about the world and to refute arguments about the supposed "joys" of slave life. Literacy meant finally having a voice in a culture of tyrannical silence and abuse. Literacy was toxic to the institution of slavery.

Slave owners were keenly aware that a literate, intelligent slave was a true oxymoron. It is nearly impossible to keep the physical body in bondage once the mind has been freed. Therefore, the necessity to prevent slaves from obtaining an education was a top priority. Knowledge was kept hidden as if it were rare jewels and rubies that required safekeeping from thieves. Indeed, one cannot disagree that an enlightened mind is a precious gift, but slaves were considered undeserving of such gifts. They certainly had no rights to the type of gift that could be passed on to others and had the potential to change lives.

White supremacy was the enemy, and a common enemy made it easy for slaves to cooperate with one another toward the goal of freedom at any cost. Slaves became well versed in the art of spying and eavesdropping and did a marvelous job of hiding their intelligence. For example, a woman in Beaufort, South Carolina, recalled that her mistress and master would verbally spell out information they didn't want her to hear. Since she was unable to read and spell, she would memorize each of the letters and repeat them promptly to her literate uncle to then decipher into words. Together they mastered the art of counterintelligence well enough to rival any Western military forces.

Educated slaves meant rebellious slaves, and they truly excelled at quiet rebellion. They were investigative journalists in every sense and worked cohesively to stay abreast of the current political debates and any changes in government legislation. No time in government policy was more critical than that of the impending Civil War between the agricultural South and industrial North.

The Civil War marked a time when anxiety and enthusiasm went hand in hand for slaves. The white men argued passionately about the intrusion of Northern Yankees into Southern matters. The discourse was angry and alluded to a potential change in slave life and the luxuries of slave ownership. The male slave sent to retrieve the mail would often hang around long enough to hear white men speaking and debating with one another about the newspaper or a letter they received. That slave would then be privy to knowledge of current affairs before his owner even read a word. On the three-mile walk back to the plantation, the mail carrier would pass on the same news on to other slaves as he traveled. Booker T. Washington referred to this as the "grape-vine telegraph." One can only marvel at such ingenuity!

The pursuit of literacy ultimately signified a method of escape. If one could eavesdrop well enough to retain information, understand that information, and then recite it to another slave who could read and possibly write, independence was certainly possible. Those brave enough to take on the pursuit of knowledge did so in the most urgent yet life-threatening secrecy. They hid in dark rooms, stole away to the forests, listened intently during Biblical read-alouds, and took books from their masters' libraries. They were renegade learners, and death would be honorable if it occurred in the pursuit of knowledge.

The risk of slaves exposing the evils of slavery was too great of a threat to go unrecognized. In defense of the business enterprise of slavery, many states enacted antiliteracy laws. It is not enough to merely intimidate slaves and beat them into submission on the plantation; there needed to be a unified effort both statewide and across state lines to ensure that slaves knew there would be serious consequences to defiance and attempting to learn. Slaves who had managed to become freedmen were particularly bothersome and were addressed promptly. For example, a law of North Carolina stated the following:

Whereas the teaching of slaves to read and write, has a tendency to excite dissatisfaction in their minds, and to produce insurrection and rebellion, to the manifest injury of the citizens of the State:

Therefore, [I] Be it enacted by the General Assembly of the State of North Carolina, and it is hereby enacted by the authority of the same, That any free person, who shall teach, or attempt to teach, any slave within this State to read or write, the use of figures excepted, or shall give or sell to such slave or slaves books or pamphlets, shall be liable to indictment in any court of record in this State…a free person of color, shall be fined, imprisoned, or whipped, at the discretion of the court, not exceeding thirty-nine lashes, nor less than twenty lashes.

[II] Be it further enacted, That if any slave shall hereafter teach, or attempt to teach, any other slave to read or write, the use of figures excepted, he or she may be carried before any justice of the peace, and on conviction thereof, shall be sentenced to receive thirty-nine lashes on his or her back. (General Assembly of the state of North Carolina, 1830–1831)

As you can see, just as slaves were conspiring to learn the written word and understand current affairs, affluent Southern whites were conspiring to keep slaves in a state of long-term submission. The list of antiliteracy laws abounded, many of which had strict statements against the general assembly of slaves during the day or night. There was the Georgia Penal Code 1833; the Code of Mississippi Article 3, Section 2 of 1823; the South Carolina Act of 1740; Missouri Law of 1847; the Virginia Revised Code of 1819; the Georgia Act of 1829; and the Alabama Act of 1831. The most vicious of these anti-literacy laws was the Louisiana Act of 1830, Section 2, which says,

> Be it further enacted; That whosoever shall make use of language, in any public discourse, from the bar, the bench, the stage, the pulpit, or in any place whatsoever; or whosoever shall make use of language in private discourse or conversations, or shall make use of signs or actions having a tendency to produce discontent among the free coloured population of this state, or to excite insubordination among the slaves therein, or whosoever shall knowingly be instrumental in bringing into this State, any paper, pamphlet, or book, having such tendency as aforesaid, shall on conviction thereof, before any court of competent jurisdiction, suffer imprisonment at hard labour, not less than three years, nor more than twenty-one years, or death, at the discretion of the court.

You read that correctly. As if thirty-nine lashes to the back wasn't terrible enough, violators in Louisiana could face up to twenty-one years in prison or be sentenced to death for having the audacity to learn. There is no question that white citizens and affluent slave owners despised the idea of educating their property. It becomes clear that the passion for learning in the black community stems from a legacy of rebellious plantation students.

Photo of an all-black classroom during segregation
with students fully engaged in the lesson.

"We Are Striving to Dwo Business on Our Own Hook": Black Schools in the Segregated South

● ● ●

They have created a national memory that dominates most thinking about the segregated schooling of African American children. In this national memory, southern African Americans were victims of whites who questioned the utility of providing blacks with anything more than a rudimentary education, who believed themselves to be bearing an unfair tax burden for the Negro schools, and who grossly underfunded African American education.

—V. SIDDLE WALKER

Whereas, knowledge is power, and an educated and intelligent people can neither be held in, nor reduced to slavery…we will insist upon the establishment of good schools for the thorough education of our children.

—PROCEEDINGS OF THE COLORED PEOPLE'S CONVENTION
OF THE STATE OF SOUTH CAROLINA, 1865

IT IS PART OF AMERICAN schools' annual rituals to pay special attention to the civil rights movement during the month of February. It is during this month that classrooms nationwide are decorated with the faces of prominent black figures who contributed substantially to the United States in every facet of modern society. In less than thirty days, public schools are expected to share the Cliff Notes version of black accomplishments. This condensed form of African American history usually results in a semirehearsed storyline that more or less says the following: "Blacks were brought to America on slave ships, worked on plantations, got freed by Abraham Lincoln's Emancipation Proclamation, lived in the segregated South, held boycotts with Rosa Parks, marched on Washington with Martin Luther King Jr., got the right to vote, and were escorted by the National Guard to newly desegregated schools. Desegregation marked the end of racism. Now we all live in harmony, have equal access to the American dream, and don't judge each other by skin color."

Although this narrative is not fully representative of the black experience in America, it is the narrative that schoolchildren are expected to memorize and regurgitate. It is a powerful and effective way of skewing the events of the past and diminishing the racial injustices of the present. When students are taught to view blacks as previous slaves with no culture or civilization prior to arriving in America, it is easy to see how many people would believe that blacks had no legitimate schools with which to educate themselves prior to desegregation. It is as though the collective American psyche believes that anything of value comes solely from whites, who are the gatekeepers of knowledge.

In contrast, a little armchair research would show anyone that although African Americans had inferior learning environments in terms of aesthetics and schoolbooks, they had an abundance of caring teachers and fully engaged parents. To this day, many scientific studies have concluded that the greatest predictor of children's future academic success, emotional health, and motivation is simply the level to which they were nurtured and loved. Children in the segregated South were truly loved and adored by their communities. Teachers frequently used their own finances to purchase additional materials and supplies for the classroom. They stayed after hours to tutor those in need. Segregated black schools that had an established presence in their communities, such as Caswell County Training School, had a plethora of extracurricular activities available to students to enrich their learning experiences. They kept records on the educational backgrounds of the parents—many of whom had not completed elementary school. They held parent-teacher conferences and worked in partnership with parents in the community to ensure their children succeeded and graduated. Yes, resources were low, but aspirations and motivations were limitless.

Initially, at the end of the Civil War, the most ambitious teachers and allies were the black Union soldiers. Former slaves proudly returned to their hometowns in flashy uniforms and with newly acquired literacy skills. They walked past their former slave owners with their heads held high and wrote letters appealing to the local governments to respect their rights as freedmen and grant them public schools to teach black children and illiterate adults. Their strongest selling point was the indisputable fact that as freedmen, they were still a prominent part of the workforce and needed a basic education in order to perform their basic work duties. One soldier by the name of Henry Mars acted as the spokesperson for his community in Kentucky and wrote to the secretary of war in May 1866 requesting permission for blacks to have basic living amenities such as grocery stores, rooming quarters for traveling blacks, and coffee shops. Even though there was talk of freedmen who had learned to read while many poor whites remained illiterate, it was truly astonishing to have former slaves writing to request spaces to cultivate their own all black public schools and communities.

Photo of Drummer Jackson before and after joining the Union. Photo reflects the massive transition from slave to freed Union soldier.

Unfortunately, the need for resources and revenue could not be ignored for long and often placed black teachers in the position of beggars. They knew that they had the ability to teach and believed in the inherent intelligence of the children being taught, but rent still needed to be paid, and many students were still without books. A teacher in Thomasville, Georgia, named Simon Ryall wrote to the Freedmen's Bureau stating, "We would be glad of sum assistance we are striving to dwo business on our own hook, but are destitute of means." The assistance they received often came in the form of a Northern white schoolteacher doing missionary work. The abolitionist missionaries arrived in the South and built single-roomed freedman's schools under the impression that the black students they taught (both young and old) would only have the mental capacity for rudimentary education encompassing simplistic and unchallenging lessons.

These same missionaries were quick to relate their surprise upon realizing that blacks had the same amount of mental capacity to learn and retain knowledge as their white counterparts. Several missionaries wrote letters to their organizations or spoke to the local newspapers about their experiences teaching in all-black schools. They each had arrived with low expectations only to be proven wrong after just a few months of working with the students. Teachers taught in classrooms with students aged five to fifty and marveled at the passion and intellect of people who literally came from nothing. Martha Kellog, a white teacher in South Carolina, stated that her students "differ like others in mental capacity—but when their degradation is remembered—their success seems almost wonderful, and as a people, they are much more intelligent then I supposed." There is power in recognizing that minorities have always had the ability to exceed all meager expectations held by whites without fail.

The black community and black families were keenly aware that their children had the potential for academic excellence but were systematically kept from leading themselves academically or flourishing financially. It wasn't until black youth attended and graduated from historically black colleges and universities that blacks felt fully equipped to demand their own public schools for children of color. One such advocate was N. Longworth Dillard, who was a recent graduate of Shaw University, a well-known college for blacks with elite professors who graduated from the most prestigious institutions across the nation.[1] Dillard was only twenty-four years old when he began canvassing his small Yanceyville, North Carolina, community to create an academically competitive Negro school. He was very ambitious and sought to grow the student body of the town's current school, where there was no water or sewage installed and no sidewalks for the townspeople to walk on.

He assumed the job of principal/teacher in 1930 and joined three other teachers to assist in educating the eighty students currently enrolled in the town's small school. Dillard used innovative tactics to gain community support for the school. He used the town newspaper to publicize PTA meetings, invite community members to school events, and acknowledged students who had achieved perfect attendance and high grade-point averages.[2] His methods were immensely effective, and within two decades, the school had grown from three teachers and 80 students to twenty-six teachers and 913 students. They also built a brand-new school called Caswell Training School, which cost well over $300,000 to construct with a full gymnasium.[3] Both Principal Dillard and the city of Yanceyville were equally proud of Caswell's accomplishments. Additionally, throughout his career, Dillard made sure he was highly involved in the lives of his students and made sure he was visible in the community at all times. He was so heavily involved that he frequently visited the homes of students and would even attend the funeral services of their family members. His overwhelming investment in his students and faculty reverberated throughout the school. Multiple students reported that their homeroom teachers were known to act as confidants and counselors to the children so that they always had a firm support system. In light of these facts, it would be modest to say that every student felt valued at Caswell. This level of genuine care led to high graduation rates and a reputation of excellence. When the Supreme Court ruled to desegregate all public schools, Caswell Training School was forced to close its doors and place the futures of its students in the hands of white teachers at a supposedly better-equipped school.

VOICES OF HOMESCHOOLING PARENTS

SABRINA'S STORY

The first time I really focused on homeschooling, a close friend and neighbor was mentioning that they were going to homeschool their children. I thought it was a great idea but didn't seriously consider homeschooling our children for a few years, until our children were six and seven years old.

We decided to homeschool for several reasons. Our primary reason was our son. We suspected for many years that our son has some type of mild developmental disorder. As soon as he started kindergarten, he would have aggressive meltdowns where he would overturn desks, throw chairs, and topple bookshelves. Once, he put his arm through a glass window. By the December holiday break, we decided to homeschool him. My husband and I were working full time, so we hired a nanny who was in school for early childhood education. She worked with him on math and language arts, took him to the park to socialize with other children, and accompanied him to art and gym classes. He excelled learning in a peaceful home environment with few distractions.

That fall, he had been diagnosed with Asperger's, an autism-spectrum disorder. So, for first grade, the school agreed to enroll him in a special class just for children with Asperger's. There were only nine children in the class and three teachers. Many of children seemed to have moderate to severe social deficiencies, and my son always felt out of place. My son was jovial and sociable and had excellent social skills. My son's primary deficiency was his ability to regulate his behavior and control his emotions.

That year in the Asperger's class, my son struggled. He did well academically but struggled within the confines of the school structure. It was heartbreaking to watch my son become increasingly depressed. We knew we had to make a change.

At this same time, our daughter was excelling academically in school. She was in the most rigorous math and reading groups in all of her classes, and she still mastered concepts very quickly. We felt she needed more challenge and rigor in her curriculum.

So, in the fall of 2012, we decided to homeschool both kids.

The most challenging part of homeschooling for our family is finding secular activities. We are African American and atheist: a super minority! We don't feel like it would be a good fit for our family values to join religious homeschool co-ops or activities. There is a growing population of secular homeschoolers in the United States, but in many US cities, religious homeschoolers dominate. So our challenge is finding secular activities while also ensuring we have minority homeschoolers to socialize with. That's important to us.

The most rewarding part of homeschooling is that I get to spend a lot of quality time with my children. I had a professional career when they were little. They went to daycare when they were babies, and most of my day was spent away from them. Now that we homeschool, I cherish every minute I get to spend with them: learning, laughing, growing.

It's really rewarding to customize their curriculums too. I love that they can do work at their ability level, regardless of whether it's at their grade level. My kids use very accelerated math which, compared to public school curricula, is one to two grade levels ahead.

I also love that my kids have a lot of influence into what they learn. If they want to study a specific person or event for social studies, then they do. If they want to read a book of their choosing for reading, then they do. Since they can focus on what they love and are interested in, I think they are that much more eager to learn, and they truly love learning.

The number-one stereotype that we battle is "the myth of socialization"! At first it used to frustrate me. Now, I just have to understand that much of America is truly ignorant about homeschoolers and homeschooling. So I try to educate people as much as I can about the socialization that my kids do get (i.e., homeschool social groups, book clubs, art classes, Girl Scouts and Boy Scouts, playing with friends in the neighborhood, socializing with cousins and other family members, etc.).

I don't define socialization as good just because children are surrounded by a lot of their peers—whom they may or may not like—who often are negatively influencing them. I define socialization by the quality of social interactions my children have. Are these children and people my children want to be around? Are they learning something from them? Are these people mature and intelligent? Are they trying to influence my children in a negative way?

My daughter has a good friend who goes to public school. This girl, let's call her Tracy, seems to have body issues, has been introduced to drugs and alcohol, and is overly interested in what's going on in pop culture instead of focusing on her schoolwork. She and my daughter like to listen to music together and play video games, but my daughter senses that school may not be the best atmosphere for kids if so much of the socialization is negative.

It's challenging to be a black homeschooler. If you live in a major city, you probably have a good percentage of black homeschoolers to socialize with, especially if you're religious. If you live in more rural areas, being a black homeschooler can be very isolating.

When we lived in North Carolina for one and a half years, there was a huge secular homeschool group. There were over three hundred families registered for this group. Typically, we were the only family of color to attend weekly events. The other homeschoolers were extremely welcoming, and we loved the group, but it could still feel isolating.

Most of our black homeschool friends are involved in predominately black homeschool coops and groups. My morals just won't allow me to sign a "declaration of faith" form before I register my kids!

My advice to aspiring homeschoolers would be that homeschooling is just like any other undertaking in life: there are pros and cons. It's best to research as many of the pros and cons beforehand so you can determine whether homeschooling is really for you and your family and so you can be prepared.

Homeschooling offers a wealth of benefits, including having evenings being solely family time since there is no homework, flexible vacation schedules, customized curriculum, eating healthier, and so on. But there are downsides. Typically, homeschool families live on one income, or the homeschool parent also works part time, which can be stressful. It can be overwhelming to spend 100 percent of your time with your kids too. It can also be challenging to juggle schoolwork, domestic duties, doctor appointments, classes, and all the activities that come along with homeschooling.

Overall, I don't know anyone who has thrown their hands up and said, "I'm done! I'm sending these kids back to school!" Homeschooling is what you make of it. I know families that homeschool seven hours per day and families that homeschool three hours per day. I know unschoolers, traditionalists, and folks who follow the Montessori model of learning. That's the nice thing about homeschooling: aside from some state requirements, you can basically do whatever meets your family's needs, and that's really nice.

YOLANDA'S STORY

We never planned to homeschool. The only homeschoolers I was acquainted with came from the Colfax book, *Homeschooling for Excellence*. I thought all homeschoolers were off-the-grid types living on self-sustaining farms. They definitely wore Birkenstocks and denim skirts.

My husband and I had worked with children for years in some capacity: daycares, afterschool programs, recreational centers, church, and finally as support staff for a local school district. Having our first child during this time, we noticed the heavy focus on testing and wanted something different. About a year or two earlier, I'd finished my master's in criminal justice, so I understood the factors affecting black males. This was also the time I began hearing people speak about the school-to-prison pipeline. I briefly worked in the prison system as well, so it wasn't so hard for us to see the need for something different.

Even with all of this, homeschooling never entered the picture. We thought more along the lines of Montessori public school or a private school. We didn't qualify for the Montessori school, and we didn't really want to pay the cost of private school. So, we enrolled our now fourteen-year-old up for kindergarten at our neighborhood school. Great place, from everything we heard from parents and children.

One day, my son and I were in the library, and I noticed a flyer advertising a homeschool informational. I attended, and the rest is history. We started meeting homeschool family after family. But none of these families were African American. I found this very active, public, and vibrant community I'd never noticed. In the early years, most of the homeschoolers I met were religious, classical-education types. So this is the style of homeschooling we modeled.

Not until we moved to Virginia did I realize homeschoolers are a varied group, and it was unnecessary to recreate school at home. Over time we became more eclectic and relaxed, and now I love the idea of following the unschooling path. But the plans some of my children have are not conducive to this method now, since they want to play college sports, and certain eligibility must be met. I've learned it's not so much the homeschool style as it is encouraging and sustaining the love of learning. We incorporate experiential-, project-, and problem-based learning as well as traditional curriculum—essentially, whatever meets their needs. We made a decision to homeschool in a way honoring our family's goals and ideals.

The first thing I'd tell African American homeschoolers is not to skip the deschooling process. We never deschooled. There was a lot of school at home in the early years. Throw in the years of educational-psychology theories, and it was probably not a lot of fun. I didn't even realize there was a need. Remember, it's a continuous process. I still need to step back at times and uncover those "schoolish" thoughts. Most of us are a product of at least twelve years of public education, and then add undergraduate and postgraduate degrees. We have to change how we think about learning. It probably won't look like what you expect.

I'd tell new African American homeschooling families to remain encouraged. Expect to be the only family of color at events unless you're in a larger city. Remember you're not alone, and there are many ways to build community in this technological age. Join African American Facebook groups. Visit African American homeschool websites. Reach out to the black community as a whole. Build a network of black homeschool and nonhomeschool moms, dads, mentors, and others in the community, no matter how small, who can relate to your family and the challenges of raising black children.

It was a long time before we met any other African American homeschoolers. I built a community of positive black people for my children. A wonderful African American family, with strong community ties, operated our dojo. A lady from our church eventually took over as the children's piano teacher. We attended various activities and events hosted by our church. Family and friends were always there to assist.

Eventually, we met African American families here and there, but nothing really intimate or long term until we moved to Virginia in 2011. We found the closer you get to an urban area, the more African American homeschool families. At least they're easier to find. This was the first time I felt truly comfortable in a group. Here were a group of women that understood institutional racism, HBCUs (Historically Black Colleges and Universities), and the struggles our children will face. We've since moved to a more rural area, so I struggle to maintain contact with these friends. So we're back to being the only black family at various activities and events. Most of our contact with black homeschool families comes through Facebook now unless we connect with our old co-op.

With that being said, we've connected with some wonderful people during our homeschool journey. Yes, we're often the only black family wherever we go. Yes, I've gotten the side eye from people surprised to see black homeschoolers. It's funny to see the reactions when slavery, the Civil War, and such topics come up. Some people really don't know what to do or say. Yes, we've made people uncomfortable so that they've either left a park date altogether or overly tried to make us welcome. I also think we're breaking barriers. I'm learning to enjoy the people we meet, knowing if we don't click, we have the choice to choose our community. I recognize a lot of people haven't been around black families in intimate settings. So I try to give people the benefit of the doubt when we first meet. But I also don't make apologies for who we are; you either accept us, or you don't.

For us, religion has played a bigger influence on our homeschooling environment than race. We do not homeschool for religious reasons, so sometimes I feel not Christian enough for certain groups but also "too Christian" for others. I prefer groups where the main focus is not religion. Homeschooling is a political statement. It can really bring out some crazy politics. People make assumptions about who you are and what you believe based on homeschooling. I like to think we defy the box, so we confuse people a little. My closest friends don't homeschool for religious reasons, so we have people who understand us. Most of the African American families we know do not homeschool for religious reasons. I think they, like us, homeschool to instill confidence and the ability for our children to come into their own without the burden of race until they're able to handle it. Plus, many of them have intimate knowledge of the educational system.

Finally, I'd advise remembering why you decided to homeschool. Try to always align your homeschool with your values. Don't try to duplicate what you read online or the family next door. I promise it's not the fairy tale you think. Step into homeschooling, and make it uniquely yours. You have the opportunity to build something new. Get away from comparisons; make homeschooling solely about your children and not your expectations. Go as fast or slow as you need. Treasure the time; all too soon it'll be gone.

Part 2: Through the Latino Lens

• • •

Yo No Tengo Soledad

Es la noche desamparo
de las sierras hasta el mar.
Pero yo, la que te mece,
¡yo no tengo soledad!

Es el cielo desamparo
si la luna cae al mar.
Pero yo, la que te estrecha,
¡yo no tengo soledad!

Es el mundo desamparo
y la carne triste va
Pero yo, la que te oprime,
¡yo no tengo soledad!

● ● ●

I Am Not Alone

The night, it is deserted
from the mountains to the sea.
But I, the one who rocks you,
I am not alone!

The sky, it is deserted
for the moon falls to the sea.
But I, the one who holds you,
I am not alone!

The world, it is deserted.
All flesh is sad you see.
But I, the one who hugs you,
I am not alone!

—Gabriela Mistral
Translated by Mary Gallwey

Animosity and Misplaced Blame

● ● ●

Give me silence, water, hope. Give me struggle, iron, volcanoes.

—Pablo Neruda

THERE'S A LOT OF ANIMOSITY surrounding the Latino community, with many people finger pointing and scapegoating an entire group of people in the name of Americanism. "If only they spoke English" is an all too common phrase that attempts to place blame on the Latino community for the failures of the American educational system. The Latino community is treated as a faceless mass of invaders with no distinctions, struggles, or ambitions. This myth must come to an end.

When it comes to the realities of life for undocumented Latino citizens, the facts are shocking. The pervasive belief that undocumented immigrants are "mooching off of the system" and are signing up by the thousands for taxpayer-funded Medicaid, food stamps, and welfare is completely unfounded. The vast majority of undocumented immigrants pay more taxes and utilize fewer government social and medical services than US citizens. The entire notion of people being "illegal" totally disregards the history of immigrant travel around the world for centuries when human beings moved freely, traded goods without barriers, and lived wherever they desired—the only exception being when kingdoms were at war for world dominance. How could the entire world have been populated over centuries if human beings only stayed in one place? Furthermore, the pilgrims who set sail on the *Mayflower* were able to take religious asylum and build new lives in America without ever having "proper documentation." Native Americans certainly did not enforce border patrol when they initially embraced the foreigners who arrived by boat. Indeed the border patrol itself was not created until 1924.

American immigration policies as we know them have been largely based on the sentiments that politicians and their constituents had toward a given ethnicity at any point in time. For instance, Chinese men were immigrating to the United States by the hundreds during the nineteenth century to build railroads in the newly developed West, but when whites became anxious at the sight of so many nonwhite faces with an unknown language, new legislation was created to block the "foreign invasion." This new legislation was called the Chinese Exclusion Act of 1882, and it was the first legislation created to stop nonwhites from immigrating to America. Unskilled European immigrants were still welcomed because industrial companies made plenty of room for these workers to find jobs and earn a living. Apparently speaking a foreign language is acceptable as long as you have the proper skin complexion. This thought process still permeates our culture today, considering that European ancestry is embraced by the dominant white culture, but African, Arab, and Mexican cultures are shamed and ridiculed. There is a very clear double standard.

When we use the term "Latino" (a person originating from Latin America) in the United States, we are actually utilizing a catchall term that encompasses six major nationalities: Mexican, Puerto Rican, Cuban, Salvadoran, Guatemalan, and Dominican. Although these six nationalities do not represent all of Latin America, they represent the most dominant Hispanic (persons originating from a Spanish-speaking country) groups found in America today. Most importantly, these six groups are the most prevalent groups found in the public school system. As of 2013, 64 percent of all Hispanics in America were Mexican, 9.5 percent Puerto Rican, 3.7 percent Cuban, 3.7 percent Salvadoran, 3.3 percent Dominican, and 2.4 percent Guatemalan.[4] These varied nationalities are bound together by a shared language and general cultural dynamics, and because Mexicans make up such a large share of the Latino American population, the Mexican culture has a strong presence as well. Despite coming from different countries of origin with a unique heritage, Latinos in America share the same plight as black Americans in terms of their low incomes, low test scores, and low graduation rates.

In terms of numbers, the Hispanic population is larger than the black population. They represent about 17 percent of the US population and are projected to account for nearly 30 percent by the year 2060.[5] Yet despite their high visibility in neighborhoods across America, Latino children struggle to attain a quality education that prepares them for future success and upward mobility. The academic progress of Latino youth has remained stagnant for decades, and Hispanics in America continue to suffer from low graduation rates, even though black youth have (slightly) increased their graduation rates within the past thirty years. These Hispanic students are not struggling academically because they are the children of immigrants but are actually native-born citizens and fully Americanized. Considering that the education crisis in America has a brown face, it's time to understand the impact of leaving so many Latino children behind.

In the book *The Latino Education Crisis*, Gándara and Contreras state the following:

> There is little dispute that successive generations of Latinos tend to outperform their parents, if those parents are very undereducated. In twenty-first century America, however, it is not sufficient for each generation to advance from, say a sixth grade education to an eighth grade education. Latinos for the most part are now stalled at the level of high school completion, with dropout rates remaining very high across generations. Only one in ten Latinos has a college degree, compared to more than one in four Whites, and more than one in three Asians. The Latino share of college degrees has not increased in more than two decades, while for all other groups the percentage of the population with degrees has increased substantially over that period.[6]

The lack of educational advancement for Latino students has serious implications for the nation as a whole. If neither the black nor Latino communities have a thriving group of educated children, the future workforce of this country is in for a serious shock. In the state of California, where the nation's largest percentage of Latino Americans reside, there is a serious risk of the state per capita income to fall by 11 percent by 2020.[7] The loss of innovation and genius is imminent when key portions of a population are underserved and undereducated.

In Search of Authenticity

The Hispanic population is plagued to a greater extent by language barriers. Surprisingly, the mastery of the English language does not lead to greater academic achievement. In fact, the inverse is often the case. Many newly immigrated students outperform their native-born Latino peers because they have a greater motivation to succeed in a new territory for their families' sakes. In addition, bilingualism aids cognitive ability, so the brain functions of newly immigrant youth are at peak levels. Conversely, native-born Latino children who have become fluent in English have a disconnect with their heritage, struggle academically, and begin to lose their Spanish language acquisition. The immense pressure for Latino students to conform to school standards has a profoundly negative effect on their collective psyche and sense of self-worth. The underlying message is that if you hate the Latino culture, you also hate the Latino child because the two do not exist separately.

This fact echoes the self-esteem-damaging techniques known collectively as subtractive schooling. This term was coined by Angela Valenzuela in her award-winning book, *Subtractive Schooling*. In her book, Valenzuela examines the culture of a predominantly Mexican school in Houston, Texas. She observed the curriculum and the interaction between teachers and students. She discovered that the public school actively and systematically subtracted Spanish language and Mexican culture from the school environment. The deliberate removal of Latino language and culture from the school environment led to resentment and a lack of motivation among the Hispanic youth.

Students read Eurocentric textbooks and stories daily. They were made to speak English as the priority language in the classroom and were expected to reduce their use of Spanish overall. They were also discouraged from doing things unique to their Mexican culture because it was believed that it undermined the Americanized school environment. In their ESL (English as a second language) classes, the bilingual education did not celebrate the native language and culture of the students but rather treated Spanish as a bad habit in need of correction. The use of high-stakes testing and lack of genuine care for students demotivated the children and led to high dropout rates. Contrary to the views of onlookers, these students did not reject education itself but rather the "schooling" they experienced on a day-to-day basis. Valenzuela states the following: "The predominantly non-Latino teaching staff see students as not sufficiently caring about school, while students see teachers as not sufficiently caring *for them*. Teachers expect students to demonstrate caring about school with an abstract, or aesthetic commitment to ideas or practices that purportedly leads to achievement. Immigrant and

US born [Latino] youth on the other hand are committed to an authentic form of caring that emphasizes relations of reciprocity between teacher and students."[8]

This sort of subtractive assimilation resonates with all minoritized people in America. In traditional schools, both public and private, we are systematically taught that Western culture is the best culture. We are taught the greatest thinkers, scientists, authors, and political figures are white and that there is a serious absence of talent and historical achievement among people of color. To be truly American means to reject all that makes you different as a person of color and instead adopt the beliefs, education, aspirations, and even the leisure pastimes of white citizens. Additionally, friendships with white students often take place on their cultural terms, not our own, in that persons of color are expected to be well versed in white American values and norms without whites being expected to know *anything* about nonwhite culture. White students are not expected to separate their heritage from their sense of self. The result is that students of color graduate knowing more about an external culture than the culture found within their own homes.

VOICES OF HOMESCHOOLING PARENTS

MONICA'S STORY

I'm a homeschooling mother of two, as well as a freelance education writer. I have two children, ages ten and twelve, and they've been schooled at home since kindergarten. Our decision to homeschool our kids was prompted by the fact that we currently live in a county that is considered to be a failed school district. The state has come in and taken over, and two of the schools in our small town were closed down completely. I'll be the first to admit that I had absolutely *no* desire to homeschool my kids, but because their education is so incredibly important to us, my husband and I felt that this was the best choice for our family. I knew several people who were (and most still are) homeschooling their children or had been homeschooled themselves. A few of these have become some of our best friends.

During our first year, I learned so much! Not only about how to teach my children but also *what* to teach them and where to find it. Since then, our school days have changed. They are continually evolving to meet the educational needs of my kids. We explore and learn and imagine every day. Like other homeschoolers, we struggle with the same stereotypes and comments from those who don't know anything about homeschooling. And we mourn that we remain the only Hispanic homeschoolers in the area.

As a Latina (my dad is from Spain, and my mother is Mexican American), I also feel the overwhelming desire to raise my children to be bilingual and bicultural. Part of this comes from my own happy childhood and a desire to share those special moments and memories with my kids. This is a lot harder for me, however, since we have moved far away from family, and our little farming community is predominantly white and black, with only a handful of Hispanic migrant workers who stay for a few months during the summer.

Apart from my desire to give my kids a happy childhood rich in culture, I know that Latino children who grow up proud of their heritage are more likely to develop "healthier behaviors" than those who don't. In a study conducted by the University of North Carolina–Chapel Hill, researchers found that these kids reported a higher self-esteem. They are also far less likely to suffer behavioral problems such as hopelessness, aggression, and substance abuse.

But it is not just their emotional well-being that drives me to pursue this path. Being bilingual has provided me with so many great opportunities that I might not otherwise have experienced. In today's global society, being bilingual is a must and can often make the difference when one of my children is being considered for a particular job or position. I am sixth generation, and while I understand Spanish perfectly and can speak it well enough, it has been a terrible struggle to pass it onto my children. Part of this stems from the fact that I married a non-Latino, and we don't have any close friends in town who speak Spanish. My spoken Spanish is also rusty from a lack of opportunity. You know the saying "Use it or lose it!" I hopped on the boat a little late, so to speak, in terms of how to raise my kids to be bilingual. I wish that I had started off using the OPOL method (One Parent One Language) from the very beginning, and so now I'm playing catch-up.

In addition to learning the language, I also strive to find ways to supplement our curriculum with cultural books, activities, and themes that reflect the richness of our heritage. We live in a small farming community, with no immersion schools or Spanish programs for small children available. So their bilingualism and biculturalism rests on my shoulders.

But the most difficult part of homeschooling has been finding materials that help us explore language and history. I couldn't find any sites or any resources for Latino homeschoolers. There were no support groups. In fact, when we started out, I was the only Latina homeschooler that I knew. So I had to start researching and even making my own materials.

As a way to share the many resources for Latino homeschoolers that I was slowly discovering through my own journey, I started the website MommyMaestra.com. The goal of my site was—and still is—to share ideas and educational resources in English and Spanish that are available for other Latino parents raising bilingual children.

Since I started MommyMaestra in 2010, it has become something much, much bigger. The people who follow are not only homeschooling parents but also parents who want to get more involved in their children's education and even bilingual-ed teachers. They speak Spanish or English; sometimes both. Some are Latino; some are married to one. And I also have non-Latino readers who have their children in dual-language programs. On MommyMaestra, my first responsibility is to my dear readers. So everything you see on my blog is related to Latino families, our children, and their education.

In my life, however, my first responsibility is to my children, and I consider their education to be of the utmost importance. Homeschooling has provided me the way to raise global citizens who are proud of themselves and their family history. And one day, I know that their learning journey will help them grow into happy, healthy, contributing members of our global society.

Part 3: The Class of 1980

• • •

Photo of an integrated class of upper elementary school students

I have a dream that one day this nation will rise up and live out the true meaning of its creed: "We hold these truths to be self-evident, that all men are created equal."

I have a dream that one day on the red hills of Georgia, the sons of former slaves and the sons of former slave owners will be able to sit down together at the table of brotherhood.

I have a dream that one day even the state of Mississippi, a state sweltering with the heat of injustice, sweltering with the heat of oppression, will be transformed into an oasis of freedom and justice.

I have a dream that my four little children will one day live in a nation where they will not be judged by the color of their skin but by the content of their character.

I have a dream today!

I have a dream that one day, down in Alabama, with its vicious racists, with its governor having his lips dripping with the words of "interposition" and "nullification"—one day right there in Alabama little black boys and black girls will be able to join hands with little white boys and white girls as sisters and brothers.

I have a dream today!

—"I Have a Dream," Martin Luther King Jr.

A Radical Experiment in Social Justice

● ● ●

United States has a long history of ignoring and breaking the
law. During the 25 or 50 years while the southern South refuses
to obey the law, what will happen to Negro children?

—W. E. B DuBois

Racial segregation in schools is an institutional complex. The
establishment and maintenance of a system of segregated educational
facilities depends upon segregation not only of pupils, but of teachers,
administrators, politicians, worshippers, and the residential segregation
of White parents from Negro parents. Segregated education depends
upon and feeds upon segregated churches, segregated businesses,
segregated recreational facilities, and segregated neighborhoods.

—Raymond W. Mack

THE CLASS OF 1980 REPRESENTS an unprecedented moment in American
history—the onset of federal desegregation. The graduating class of 1980
was the first class of graduating high school seniors who spent their entire

kindergarten through high school years in fully integrated classrooms. They were the lovechildren of a revolution. The black, white, and Latino children who entered kindergarten in the fall of 1967 lived the daily lives envisioned by the Freedom Fighters and the prolific activists of the civil rights movement. They were the recipients of a gift given by the Supreme Court decision in *Brown v. Board of Education*. Separate was no longer considered equal; in fact, separate would no longer be legal.

In the landmark case of *Brown v. Board of Education of Topeka, Kansas* (1954), the US Supreme Court put an end to the long-standing rule of "separate but equal." The notion of "separate but equal" was made famous in the case of *Plessy v. Ferguson* (1896) in which the Court formerly ruled that state laws requiring separate public facilities for whites and nonwhites was constitutional, as long as they were equal in function. However, it soon became evident that *none* of the separate facilities for minorities were equal to those of whites, and the idea of separate but equal was inherently *unequal*.

Brown v. Board of Education was the catalyst for sweeping changes in the national public education system. It ushered in a new vision for American education that was much greater than the federally mandated changes to school funding allocations. The urgency to integrate schools nationwide meant that many schools needed to compete to attract white students to predominantly black and Latino communities with public schools that were labeled as "Mexican schools" or "negro schools." This competition led to the creation of magnet schools that sought to attract new students with specialized programs in technology, linguistics, multicultural education, and the arts.

For the first time in history, educators were teaching to fully integrated classrooms with children from both sides of the railroad tracks, and white teachers could interact with students of color on a daily basis. The class of 1980 was the grand social experiment in desegregation and would prove once and for all that minority students were as intelligent, talented, and ambitious as their white counterparts. It also proved that white children could form meaningful friendships with minority students.

The kindergarteners of 1967 sat in the same classrooms, laughed and played together in the schoolyard, and ate lunch in the same cafeterias. Once they reached high school, they became teammates on athletic teams or chanted together on cheerleading squads. They marched together in the school marching band or performed in school plays with a multicultural cast. They were best friends and enemies. They were lovers and competitors. They were regular school kids, who happened to come in different-colored skins.

These students represented the promise of a new era and a new future in America, a future of inclusion, acceptance, and a tolerance for differences. When the class of 1980 threw its graduation caps in the air, America was forever changed. Or so we thought…

In the book *Both Sides Now,* Amy Stuart Wells and researchers at the University of California sought to find various graduates from the class of 1980 throughout the country and answer the following questions: "How do graduates of racially mixed schools understand their school experience and its effect on their lives—their racial attitudes, educational and professional opportunities, personal relationships, and social networks? And how did the policy context of their experiences shape these understandings?"[9] In other words, "Where are they now?" and "Was the massive integration of schools impactful?"

The front view of Topeka High school in Topeka, Kansas,
where *Brown v. Board of Education* originated

To find the answers to these questions, researchers contacted 268 alumni from six high schools across the country. They chose to sample towns and districts with significant desegregation plans in terms of size, region, racial and ethnic makeup of the general population and the students, social class of residents, and the policies by which the districts were desegregated.[10] They also chose alumni based on variations in racial makeup, academic success, socioeconomic status, the distance of their residences from schools, and their involvement in high school activities.[11] Overall, the researchers went to great lengths to ensure that the results of their evaluation would be fully representative of the demographics within American society as a whole. The chosen schools with representative alumni for the class of 1980 were the following:

1. Austin High School, Austin, Texas (Austin Independent School District). Desegregated via majority-to-minority transfers from several areas. Racial makeup during the mid-1970s: 15 percent African American, 19 percent Hispanic, 66 percent white.

2. Dwight Morrow High School, Englewood, New Jersey (Englewood Public Schools). Desegregation by receiving white students from the neighboring town of Englewood Cliffs via sending-receiving plan. In addition to the Englewood Cliffs students, Dwight Morrow enrolled all public school students from the racially diverse town of Englewood. Busing and student reassignment began at the elementary level in the Englewood Public Schools at that time. Racial makeup of Dwight Morrow during the mid-1970s: 57 percent African American, 7 percent Hispanic, 36 percent white.

3. John Muir High School, Pasadena, California (Pasadena Unified School District). Desegregated originally by drawing from several diverse attendance areas and in the 1970s via mandatory busing. Racial makeup during the late 1970s: 50 percent African American, 12 percent Hispanic, 34 percent white, 4 percent Asian/Pacific Islander.

4. Shaker Heights High School, Shaker Heights, Ohio (Shaker Heights City School District). Desegregated as the only high school in a district experiencing an influx of African American students from Cleveland. Efforts were made in Shaker Heights to integrate neighborhoods, and student reassignment began at the elementary level. Racial makeup during the 1970s: 39 percent "minority" (mostly African American) and 61 percent white.

5. Topeka High School, Topeka, Kansas (501 School District). Desegregated via assigned attendance areas; student reassignment began at the elementary and junior high levels. Racial makeup during the 1970s: 20 percent African American, 8 percent Hispanic, 69 percent white, 1.4 percent American Indian, 1.4 percent Asian.

6. West Charlotte High School, Charlotte, North Carolina (Charlotte-Mecklenburg School District). Desegregated via court order that created a district-wide desegregation plan and reassigned students from white high schools to this historically black high school. Racial makeup during the 1970s: 48 percent African American and 52 percent white.[12]

The results of their investigation proved to be equally complex and disheartening.

It was true that the students thoroughly enjoyed the experience of attending a racially diverse school, but the experience within the school walls did not translate into their day-to-day lives *outside* of the school. The students were still faced with segregated neighborhoods in which the typical hang-out spots for teenagers as well as places of worship were divided.[13]

Within the schools, many of the white administrators and teachers found it difficult to fully embrace interactions with children of color since those interactions were against their will and were instead the will of the government. This internal conflict was seen through unfair punishments and dismissive attitudes toward students of color, as well as a reluctance to grant minorities access to honors and AP courses.[14] The public schools were also guilty of "tracking" minority students into vocational programs based solely on subjective observations and conversations, even when students or parents requested more challenging coursework. The teachers and administrators had internal stereotypical views about the intellectual capacity of minoritized students. These students were denied access to the rigorous courses and valuable information thought to prepare students for college through no real fault of their own but rather due to the assumptions of school authority figures.

Additionally, it was during the years of 1967–1980 that "multicultural education" was created. Teachers and administrators shied away from engaging in any racial discussions or speaking in depth about black, Latino, Native American, or Asian activists or revolutionaries or their shared struggles for equality. Instead, teachers created a "multicultural" curriculum that revolved around ritualistic, holiday celebrations found around the world with brief mentions of some famous figures. In truth, the experiences of the class of 1980 created the new standard for what is now the norm of race relations in America—"colorblindness."

The colorblind ideology was created as a method of school policy that removed race from the educational curriculum as a means of "keeping the peace" and focusing on the individuals instead of their collective racial backgrounds. Teachers and administrators nationwide subscribed to the belief that they "did not see color" in regards to their students but instead saw each child as a unique person. Colorblind policies abounded from the 1970s onward, and policy makers *still* subscribe to the belief that by avoiding any legislation based on racial equality, the issue of racism will eventually go away. This belief system can be seen as recently as 2007 in the US Supreme Court cases of *Parents Involved in Community Schools v. Seattle School District No.1* and *Meredith v. Jefferson County Board of Education*, when the Court ruled that school integration plans that take the racial identity of the individual students into account when assigning them to schools is *un*constitutional.[15]

Schools routinely reserve discussions of "racism and ethnicity" for the annual designated day or month of ethnic celebration, while simultaneously keeping the bulk of historical discussion focused on white male achievements. American history is not treated as a tapestry of varied experiences and struggles but rather as the story of a country that was once overwhelmingly white and Christian prior to World War II, after which time other ethnicities immigrated into the country and brought diversity. The minoritized populations within the country and their respective cultures are treated merely as a welcomed addition to the great American melting pot and not the foundation of the country itself.

During the initial years of forced integration, white children bused to predominantly minority neighborhoods became immersed in the world of black and Latino culture and easily found commonalities. The minority students who were sent to affluent, white suburbs were able to see the differences in social status and customs and also gained new insight into the values of social mobility. Although their children attended integrated schools where they made friends of other backgrounds, the parents themselves were in communication solely on a superficial level, if at all. It was as if the children's schools were time machines to an unknown future that was in bold contrast to the streets they rode their bicycles on or the pizza joints they ate at after school.

It was this bold contradiction that prevented the white graduates of 1980 from embracing integration and diversity across the board. Many spoke fondly of times spent with mixed crowds in extracurricular activities and the comradery that it created. Unfortunately these Monday through Friday school-based friendships did not carry over to the weekends. Racism saturated the academic environment as well as the communities surrounding the utopian mixed-raced schools. The stories of Larry Rubin of Dwight Morrow High School and Henry Delane of Topeka High School sum up these experiences perfectly.

Larry grew up in Englewood, New Jersey, and attended middle-class, mixed-race schools that included students from both ends of the socioeconomic spectrum. He even worked during the summers in high school while his affluent friends went on teen tours or to sleep-away camps.

In contrast, once he graduated, got married, and had children, Larry did not think twice about enrolling his children in a predominantly white school within a mostly white neighborhood (the exception being a handful of Asian and Indian families). There was little to no contact with African Americans or Hispanics of any kind. The book states the following:

Life was good for Larry and his family. Like so many White, upper-middle-class families, they had benefited from the shifts in the American economy since the early 1980s—twenty five years in which those in the highest income bracket, the "fortunate fifth," made more money and acquired wealth much faster than everyone else. They had a home that would fit comfortably in the pages of *House Beautiful*, a well-equipped minivan, and the American Dream of a large plot of land in a safe and secure suburb, far removed from the most vexing social problems of large cities and poorer communities.[16]

Yes, Larry's life postgraduation has been a staircase of opportunity and wealth accumulation. But Larry was keenly aware of his children's lack of experiences with other races as well as his own regrets about the loss of friendships, saying, "I have such warm feelings and memories of being with all these people, and we didn't save any of it...I am not friends with them now...I think I went off into my white world...people live lives for the most part along color."

Henry Delane and his family had always been a part of the black community where he was born and raised. He attended Topeka High School in Topeka, Kansas, which was located in the historic city made famous by the *Brown v. Board of Education* court case. He was one of a few black students enrolled in the upper-track classes and spoke of his resentment toward the teachers and administrators who did not incorporate different racial perspectives into the curriculum. On the subject of history class, he said, "We never talked about, you know, accomplishments of...blacks in history...but you sure as hell would talk about George Washington."

Henry experienced many microaggressive and subtly racist pranks during his high school years, which he believes thoroughly prepared him for life after graduation. He attended a predominantly white university, lives in a predominantly white neighborhood, enrolled his kids in a predominantly white public school, and works as the vice president of a bank not far from Topeka. However, he still has to deal with unwelcoming white neighbors who refuse to wave at him or pseudofriendly white neighbors who say they'll invite his family over for a barbeque. In regard to the barbeque, Henry stated simply, "We've been here since 1997, haven't been to a barbeque yet." His family's social life revolves around the local black church, where he is very involved, and none of the family's social activities involve white neighbors or coworkers. The social institutions he encountered postgraduation were still staunchly segregated by race.

As these two stories illustrate, the extent of the friendships formed and experiences shared within integrated schools did not translate well into the reality of racially segregated social lives that remained a staple throughout their school years and continues to this day. The class of 1980 was prolific in its achievement of school integration and mixed-race friendships. However, they graduated with whimsical ideas of unity and tolerance yet had no practical methods for implementing them.

Part 4: Traditional Schooling

• • •

A group of students outside of Normandy High School just moments
after the bell rang at the end of school in Wellston, Saint Louis
County, MO. 2014, Photo by Trymaine Lee for MSNBC.

I sit down, dreading the upcoming day
Asia barges into the room like a battering ram
loud and destructive
as always her clothes are boa constricting
and she walks with a practiced switch…
when the door opens again my friend Mollie walks in
usually he has a smile of sunshine and walks lightly with a grasshopper spring
in his steps
today his steps are like lead
there is no smile, only pain in his irises
I know a lot about Mollie
His father has been playing peek-a-boo with his childhood since he was born
and his stepfather is an alcoholic with drunken fists of non-discretion
he was birthed into a world he wasn't ready for
where battering punches take the place of love
just then Duma walks into class
he has the rough, violent, tongue of a sailor
when he enters the classroom he wanders around like a nomad
deliberately getting on everyone's nerves…
Duma is a motherless child who says bitch a lot
he always talks about how he doesn't trust women
he thinks of them as butterflies beautiful and majestic, but they don't tend to
stay around long enough
About halfway through class Jonathon walks in
today his bloodshot eyes are droopy and he has a dazed look
he only comes once a month or when we have a sub
and when that happens he shoots dice in the back with Duma and Daniel
—"Bored in 1st Period," Obasi Davis

Living in Two Worlds

● ● ●

I taught for thirty years in some of the worst schools in Manhattan,
and in some of the best, and during that time I became an expert in
boredom. Boredom was everywhere in my world, and if you asked the
kids, as I often did, why they felt so bored, they always gave the same
answers...teachers are themselves products of the same twelve-year
compulsory school programs that so thoroughly bore their students,
and as school personnel they are trapped inside structures even more
rigid than those imposed upon the children. Who, then, is to blame?

—JOHN TAYLOR GATTO

MANY OF US HAVE FOND memories of public school. We made friends, had
our first kiss, went on memorable field trips, and enjoyed pep rallies. Some
of our favorite films depict life experiences in public school—*Pretty in Pink*,
The Breakfast Club, *American Pie*, and so on. We were able to catch glimpses
of ourselves in the characters portrayed on screen. We were able to laugh at
the all-too-common dull teachers like the one in *Ferris Bueller's Day Off*. We
could sing along with the actors in *Grease* and reminisce on the power of
friendship. We laughed at the crazy antics of the rich and popular girl cliques

in *Clueless* and *Mean Girls*. We fantasized about being athletes like the football players in *Friday Night Lights* or the ugly duckling who became the center of attention in *She's All That*. Indeed, Hollywood has done a great job of creating films that highlight the happy and bittersweet moments of the high school and the public school experience. However, there's something we're neglecting to mention here—all of these movies with their all-star casts are all white at nearly all-white schools. We even have a term for the one or two black or Latino faces we see on screen—"token," meaning it's a half-assed attempt to portray "diversity" on screen worthy of a cheap token for good effort.

Now let's examine the actual narrative found in the black and Latino high school movies. If you do a very brief analysis of films like *Lean on Me*, *Stand and Deliver*, *Dangerous Minds*, *Freedom Writers*, *Coach Carter*, *Light It Up*, and others, one central theme is revealed—the struggling school. The struggling school is the stereotypical urban and low-income school filled with black and brown faces. We are bombarded with images of dilapidated buildings, apathetic students, overworked teachers, outdated textbooks, and criminal activity. The stories of the struggling school are inspirational tales about students who excel academically, athletically, or creatively with the help of a passionate teacher, despite their negative environments. In contrast, when we think of predominantly white schools, "struggle" is the furthest thing from our minds. More often than not we think of high school pranks, athletic teams, underage drinking, and teen romance—the only exception being teen horror films. It's wonderful to depict images of minority children succeeding "against all odds," but why is that narrative only reserved for children of color?

There is an uncomfortable truth about academic success being a basic right for white children but an ongoing fight for children of color—especially in low-income areas. This negative perception of predominantly black and Latino schools has muddled the line between reality and fiction. It has gotten to the point that white families living in well-kept, racially diverse neighborhoods will still drive several miles in order to send their children to predominantly white schools, because they wholeheartedly believe those schools are better. There is little genuine research done into comparing test scores and graduation rates between neighborhoods, but rather white parents base their decisions on word-of-mouth advice from real estate agents and gossip from other white families. This "white flight" has created a resegregation of endemic proportions that spiked heaviest during the 1990s. Not since before the 1960s have American schools been this segregated.

In the book *The Shame of a Nation: The Restoration of Apartheid Schooling in America*, author Jonathan Kozol explores schools in the South Bronx of New York. The South Bronx has a long history of being the epicenter for low-performing schools filled with low-income minority students. Schools in this area frequently get labeled as Title 1 schools, which means they need extra assistance in order to adequately meet state and national education standards. On the subject of resegregation in schools, Kozol notes what many people of color have known for decades:

> One of the most disheartening experiences for those who grew up in the years when Martin Luther King and Thurgood Marshall were alive is to visit public schools today that bear their names, or names of other honored leaders of the integration struggles that produced the temporary progress that took place in the three decades Brown, and to find how many of these schools are bastions of contemporary segregation. It is even more disheartening when schools like these are not in segregated neighborhoods but in racially mixed areas in which

the integration of a public school would seem to be most natural, and where, indeed, it takes a conscious effort on the part of parents or of school officials in these districts to avoid the integration option that is often right at their front door.

In a Seattle neighborhood, for instance, where approximately half the families were Caucasian, 95 percent of students at Thurgood Marshall elementary were Black, Hispanic, Native American, or of Asian origin. An African American teacher at the school told me of seeing clusters of White parents and their children on the corner of a street close to the school each morning waiting for a bus that took the children to a school in which she believed that the enrollment was predominantly white.

It's a running joke in the black community that all streets and schools named after civil rights leaders are always located in the hood. Apparently there's more truth to that joke then we'd like to admit. The legacies of our honored civil rights leaders seem to be the integration of *public spaces* such as parks, restaurants, theaters, libraries, and so on as opposed to the full integration of American lives across racial lines. Minoritized populations in America only make up a small percentage of residents in prosperous suburban neighborhoods, own only 0.5 percent of the nation's wealth, and children of color are being lumped together into a low-functioning school system whose problems get ignored by the general public.

CHARTER SCHOOLS MEAN BUSINESS

Contrary to popular belief, charter schools are public schools that receive public money, but they do not have to follow the same accountability systems.

They are best likened to public schools with private school rights. The idea of charter schools have their origins in Milton Friedman's vision for "school choice" for families and Albert Shanker's belief that removing the restraints of school bureaucracy will bring competition and innovation to education. These public schools select students via lottery and are only held accountable for the standards and goals detailed within the charter. The charter contract becomes the sole decision-making reference that determines whether or not a charter school gets a contract extension or is closed down due to insufficient progress.

Unlike traditional public schools, charter schools have autonomy in five key areas:

1. Time—they can have a longer school day or week;
2. Money—they choose how to spend the public money and donations they receive;
3. People—the school determines qualifications and requirements for hiring and firing staff;
4. Policy—they are regulated by a charter that outlines accountability and initiatives; and
5. Governance—a board of directors helps make decisions without district oversight.

A "charter" can be best described as a performance contract that charter schools have that outlines the mission, goals, and indicators of performance of the school. The charter generally lasts three to five years and can be used as a basis to close charter schools that do not meet their stated performance goals (Stoelinga 2016). This charter serves as a foundation of operations and organization for the charter school.

Charter schools were conceived as an idea by the former president of the American Federation of Teachers Albert Shanker as a way of allowing educators to have greater influence over the curriculum and daily activity of the schools in which they taught.

However, charter schools have evolved into a system of corporate- and nonprofit-owned schools with far less freedom and influence given to teachers. They have kept most of the day-to-day practices and financial decisions out of public view. There have been just as many experts promoting charter schools as there have been experts denouncing them. Charter schools have become a controversial and divisive topic in modern American public education.

Arguments that applaud the charter school movement tend to cite the high graduation rates and competitive test scores found at many of the nation's charter schools. They also point out that charter schools are a good alternative for students who would otherwise be stuck at a chronically failing public school. In contrast, critics of charter schools speak of the low percentage of students being served by charter schools and the imbalanced high concentration of charter schools in a few select cities as well as their lack of contagious innovation. There is still heated debate as to whether or not they have any perceivable innovation at all. I want to highlight the current state of the charter-school movement because of their disciplinary policies, exploitation of low-income minority neighborhoods, and strong ties to corporate entities. These schools use unprecedented methods for achieving high test scores as "proof" that they are doing the most good for children of color.

There's a nonprofit organization called Character Lab that is dedicated to helping teachers keep score cards of students' behavior patterns or "character growth." Using a tool called the Character Growth Card, teachers can select which category they wish to score children and rate them on a scale of "almost never" to "almost always." The options are as follows:

Curiosity—a strong desire to know or learn something
Gratitude—appreciation for the benefits we receive from others and
a desire to
reciprocate
Grit—perseverance and passion for long term goals
Growth Mindset—understanding that intelligence can be developed
Optimism—being hopeful about future outcomes combined with
agency to shape
that future
Purpose—being driven by something larger than yourself
Self-Control—controlling one's own responses so they align with
short and long
term goals
Social/Emotional Intelligence—understanding feelings and using
them to inform
actions
Zest—an approach to life that is filled with excitement and energy

Yes, you read that right: fucking zest. Can you imagine going to a parent-teacher conference and having the teacher say, "I'm sorry to tell you this, but Keisha and Rafael have been lacking in the 'zest' department..." The categories for scoring these children are a slap in the face of minorities throughout this country who know that no matter what your personal level of optimism, grit, and sense of purpose, there are structural issues outside of your control as an individual that have a tremendous impact on your future success. Structural racism and poverty greatly decrease one's life chances. If an employer decides to fire a person of color over a white employee during layoffs, if a minority student can't afford college tuition, or if a person of color can't secure a home loan—it doesn't matter what that person's personal sentiments were because there were factors outside of his or her control that prohibited the individual from reaching his or her highest potential. It's a sickening burden to place on the shoulders of children that their desire to succeed will guarantee them future success similar to their white peers living in better zip codes.

Now I'm sure you must be thinking that there's no way this has become mainstream, but think again. This scorecard and discipline-tracking method is used in the famous KIPP charter schools and is even promoted on their site. In other words, they are ~~embarrassed~~ thrilled to have the ability to measure children not only by aptitude in terms of standardized-test performance but also in the intangible traits such as the willingness to succeed, optimistic out-look, ability to resolve conflict with others, and the ability to be an all-around "peppy" robot. The most troubling thing about this is that a group of edu-cated adults thought that it would be a good idea to measure these children in such an invasive manner. Teachers give out literal kudos to students appear-ing to be excited about the highly disciplined environment the KIPP schools are known for, as well as their ability to engage with others in a measurable, teacher-approved way. Why is this level of scrutiny necessary?

This is a serious, unprecedented, and disheartening level of disregard for ethics in the classroom. The key thing to keep in mind here is that we are talking about impressionable children who spend eight hours a day with trusted adults, who in turn exploit them by forcefully molding them into a series of numbers and markings on a page. These children are being actively trained like animals to do tricks for a reward. The reward is a letter grade and a numerical score on a sheet of paper.

How many adults would be okay with their employers scoring them on something as subjective as their *character*? You would automatically cry foul because your employer's opinion of you will be based solely on the portion of yourself that you reveal in the work environment. We all wear many hats as individuals. It would be unfair to assume that your boss could understand you as a whole person unless you spent extensive time with him or her outside of the workplace. So why do this to kids? It seems a bit far-fetched to believe that a teacher could properly grade the true character of twenty kids in a classroom with four classes a day. Her selections on the scorecard would be superficial, one dimensional, and ill informed. Furthermore, what are the repercussions for children who score "below average" in character? Will their parents be given the assistance needed to better their home lives, or will those students simply be pushed out of school for being bad influences? My intuition tells me it's the latter. What is the message we are sending these children, and what sort of future adults are we grooming? This is a very real example of disingenuous care for the well-being of children.

DOLLA DOLLA BILLS, Y'ALL

Money, money, money. There is so much money to be made off struggling, low-income schools in need of reform. The great reformers come with a laser focus on long-term profits and short-term gains. They are governed by business leaders with pockets full of private, corporate donations. "There is a continuum of disingenuous marketing schemes sold under the guise of charitable giving," said Arnold Fege, director of public engagement and advocacy for the Public Education Network and founder of Public Advocacy for Kids. "For many givers, their heart's in the right place, but it has become too much about publicity. And education becomes a charity, not a civic endeavor."[17] Indeed, public education (especially in the form of charter schools) has become the bridge that connects corporate profits to charitable donations. Many corporations are running to the public school sector as a means of meeting their philanthropic donation quota as well as securing future consumers. School buses and athletic fields are sporting company logos, and cafeterias serve brand-name fast foods. In addition, many hedge funds and corporations like Walmart use their private foundations to funnel massive financial contributions to charter schools and form close relationships with the schools' boards of directors. These corporate entities form ~~educational mafias~~ educational management organizations (EMOs) and open charter schools in low-income areas that serve black and brown youth. Their tactics are controversial, but the financial rewards and tax incentives for the wealthy are plentiful.

The Walton Family Foundation, a philanthropic foundation for Walmart, cosponsors an annual symposium called Bonds and Blackboards: Investing in Charter Schools that teaches hedge funds and legislators about the financial gains of the charter-school movement. They invite top-name heavy hitters in the financial realm and sweet-talk political figures in order to secure their influence over public school policy initiatives and legislative decisions. Attendees for the year 2015 included JP Morgan, Bank of America Merrill Lynch, Prudential Investments, and Wells Fargo.[18] "Walton has subsidized an entire charter school system in the nation's capital," the *New York Times* reported, "helping to fuel enrollment growth so that close to *half of all public school students in the city* now attend charters" (emphasis mine).[19] The *New*

York Times is not the only group taking notice of the efforts to privatize public education. The organization called the Washington Park Project recently wrote a paper fully detailing the dark side of the charter school movement, stating that "New York State is plagued by legal corruption: campaign contributions and outside spending explicitly designed to buy policy outcomes. In 2014, a tiny group of powerful hedge fund executives, representing an extreme version of this corruption, spent historic amounts of money in order to take over education policy."[20]

If the goal is to turn schools into a replica of Wall Street, then these billion-dollar corporations have established a firm method of gauging their profit margins—high stakes testing. Standardized test effectively attach a bottom-line number of value to every student and potentially every teacher. Teachers are frequently videotaped and made to dedicate innumerable hours to filing paperwork for administrators to then share with their advisory boards. Perhaps someday soon, there will be shares of charter schools readily available for purchase. After all, the business of education is a high-demand, high return, and low risk financial investment. Financial portfolios can only be strengthened by buying stocks in the education realm—as long as standardized tests and teacher evaluations can be numbered and measured, it's a sound investment. Wait, what were we discussing again? Oh right, the *children*. See how easy it is to completely disregard the humanity of the children involved in these financial decisions? Yeah, it's unsettling.

These groups collectively operate under the vague term of "reformers" and make grandiose statements about their commitment to education and the future of public schools. Hedge fund managers have no oversight or scrutiny in terms of their financial decisions, nor do they have to reveal their motivations and desired outcomes to the public. The Department of Education still labels charter schools as public schools, but are they really public considering the majority of their decision making is done in private boardrooms? It appears that the only thing truly public about charter schools are the taxpayer dollars being used to pay for operating facilities and the major tax breaks companies receive for "donating" funds to these privatized schools.

DISCIPLINE FIRST, OBEDIENCE SECOND, AND EDUCATION EVENTUALLY

Many of the modern minority public schools have become well-photographed academies of discipline. The children are dressed in neatly pressed uniforms, can recite school mission statements on demand, and never speak out of turn. They have brand names like KIPP (Knowledge is Power Program), Success Academies, YES Prep, Uplift, BASIS, and AIM. The students walk in single-file lines, have silent lunches, and sometimes have silent recess. The administrators firmly teach to the test and subscribe to a doctrine of discipline called "zero tolerance." Zero-tolerance policies place classroom management at the center of school productivity and allow for students to be written up and suspended for the smallest infractions. How small? Well, a student can be suspended for staring into space, talking too loudly, slouching, having an attitude, and other behaviors teachers consider annoying disruptive. Zero-tolerance policies extend beyond the classroom as well, because for many public schools, uniform standards are equally unrelated imperative to school success. An eighth grader who attended UP Academy, a famous group of schools by the UP Education Network, shared the following story:

Traumatized. That's the word my friends and I use when we talk about our school. It really scarred us. We were so used to freedom, like being able to walk to lunch in groups. All of a sudden, we were treated like children. Our lockers were taken away. Instead we had cubbies in our classrooms. We were like "cubbies? Are you joking???" We weren't allowed to transition; our teachers transitioned. We stayed in the same room, in our chairs for 8 hours a day. We only moved when we went to lunch. We had to line up in a particular order and if you weren't in the right order or if somebody was talking, you'd have to go back to the classroom and start again. There was one time when we missed lunch because we went through this process fifteen times.

They said that discipline led to academic success. They were incredibly strict about the uniform and we weren't used to that. In the morning when we walked in we had to lift up our pants so that they could make sure we were wearing the socks we were allowed to wear, check to make sure we had a belt and that we had the school logo on our shirts. They'd say "if you don't have the logo, we're not going to let you in. We're going to send you to the dean's office and you're going to get a uniform and you're going to get out-of-school detention." What really bothered me was that even if you had an excuse, like your uniform was in the laundry, and your mom called, they would still send you to the dean's office…

The white teachers were so into the system. They loved it. The Hispanic teachers were the only ones who understood us. We connected with them because they didn't like the system either. There was one Hispanic teacher who was very honest with us. She'd enforce the rules and give us demerits and detentions, and tell us that if we disrespected her, she was going to disrespect us back. She was very firm about that. But she always told us how much she hated the system. All of the Hispanic teachers left; they didn't want to work there."[21]

Therein lies yet another a reason for minority teachers to walk away from schools, as if budget cuts, poor infrastructure, lack of resources, and overcrowded classrooms weren't enough of a deterrence—they now have to stomach unjust disciplinary practices. These children are stripped of their personhood both literally and figuratively in the name of supposed academic success. This disregard for childhood and intolerance for childlike behavior begins in kindergarten. There are reported cases of kindergarteners being suspended up to sixteen times within a single school year.[22] Suspensions can last one to three days or even longer, at the school's discretion. This method of discipline is disproportionately affecting learning-disabled and minority students. Students of color and special-needs children are being harshly disciplined for minor infractions to the extent that they become marked as "problem children" or are effectively pushed out of the school altogether.

These policies neither benefit the students nor distinguish between common childlike behavior, special-needs challenges, and class disruption. It has even been reported that charter school administrative staff members have drafted lists of students who have "got to go" due to constant infractions.[23] Once a child has been listed as such, the school administration works tirelessly to frustrate the child and exhaust the parents (through constant midday school visits) into withdrawing the child. One has to ask what sort of validity a discipline program has that allows for a five-year-old to be suspended and delights in pushing students out of school!

Unfortunately the zero-tolerance policies do not guarantee that public school students will do better academically; in most cases, they get minimal increases in test scores, and in some cases, they actually do worse. In regard to the few charter schools with high test scores, rampant fraud and questionable ethics have come to light. Zero-tolerance policies have their origins in the broken-windows theory introduced in 1982 by James Q. Wilson and George L. Kelling. The broken-windows theory is actually a criminological theory for redirecting criminal behavior by penalizing the smallest offenses in the belief that small offenses lead to more severe criminal acts, antisocial behavior, and vandalism. Wilson and Kelling explained the broken-windows analogy in this way:

> At the community level, disorder and crime are usually inextricably linked, in a kind of developmental sequence. Social psychologists and police officers tend to agree that if a window in a building is broken and is left unrepaired, all the rest of the windows will soon be broken. This is as true in nice neighborhoods as in rundown ones...serious street crime flourishes in areas in which disorderly behavior goes unchecked. The unchecked panhandler is, in effect, the first broken window. Muggers and robbers, whether opportunistic or professional, believe they reduce their chances of being caught or even identified if they operate on streets where potential victims are already intimidated by prevailing conditions.[24]

Yes, these schools are utilizing police and prison tactics to control the behavior of schoolchildren. Unfortunately, the idea of properly disciplining "ethnic" students in order to educate them is as old as minority public education itself. When missionaries and abolitionists first began doing charity work in the form of educating newly freed slaves and indigenous people, they all collectively felt as though proper discipline would be needed in order make them civilized. The founder of Hampton Institute and mentor to Booker T. Washington, Samuel Chapman Armstrong, was a missionary turned educator and strongly believed that training blacks to be *civilized* would be more difficult than teaching them. In 1877, he wrote, "His worst master is still over him—his passions. This he does not realize. He does not see 'the point' of life clearly; he lacks foresight, judgment, and hard sense. His main trouble is not ignorance, but deficiency of character...the question with him is not one of brains, but of right instincts, of morals and of hard work."[25]

The same logic applied to the teaching of Native Americans. Carlisle Indian Industrial School was established in 1879 by Richard Henry Pratt. Pratt was a veteran army officer who fought in the Indian Wars; he also captured and imprisoned Native Americans during that time and felt that he gained great insight into the educational needs of the indigenous people. He decided that he was equipped and enthusiastic enough to teach indigenous children how to assimilate themselves into to civilized society. He used passionate phrases like "tame the wild Indian" to describe his ambitions. The Carlisle School did a great job of removing "savage" tendencies from the indigenous children it educated and dressing them in proper Euro-American clothing in effort to have them embrace white culture. However, when legislators noticed that assimilation wasn't happening fast enough, they enacted the Dawes Act of 1887, which stripped Native Americans of their communal lands and instead gave them individual plots of land to farm, knowing that property ownership and farming was against indigenous cultural practices. Native Americans had their tribal affiliations removed, and the Dawes Act allowed the United States to seize the majority of land previously owned by native tribes.

A new version of the Carlisle School emerged in 1996 in the form of the American Indian Public Charter School (AIPCS), which serves middle-school minority students in Oakland, California. Taken over by Ben Chavis in 2000, the school uses verbal and psychological abuse to attain high test scores. They recruited favorable teachers with phrases like "we are looking for hard working people who believe in free market capitalism…multicultural specialists, ultra liberal zealots and college-tainted oppression liberators need not apply."[26] Zero-tolerance discipline reaches new lows at this school, where misbehaving students have had their heads shaved, nonwhite students are called "darkies," public humiliation and verbal abuse are the norm, and girls have been made to clean the boys' bathroom as punishment.[27]

Why has this school been allowed to remain standing? The answer is simple. It is a beacon of academic excellence. Their controversial discipline tactics along with the use of Saturday school and mandatory summer school have placed AIPCS among the highest-scoring schools in the state of California. California utilizes the Academic Performance Index to rank schools on a scale of 0 to 1,000. The state average for middle and high school students is about 750, and low income schools score around 650. The American Indian Public Charter school boasts a score of 967.

Though the school's methods are questionable, the results are measurable and have gained praise from financial backers like the Koret Foundation, a Bay Area group that has given more than $100,000 in grants to American Indian Charter School. "They really should be the model for public education in the state of California," said Debra England of the Koret Foundation. "What I will never understand is why the world is not beating a path to their door to benchmark them, learn from them and replicate what they are doing."[28] Although Ben Chavis was removed from the board of directors when financial audits revealed he embezzled millions in taxpayer funds, AIPCS has grown to become the American Indian model with a total of three charter schools serving low-income minority schools.

Voices of Homeschooling Families

Shala's Story

I have been homeschooling my son, Ky, who is nine, for over a year now. Although I had heard about homeschooling for years around the way, I actually had a conversation about it when he was about seven. A parent from our football team told me that she was a homeschooling parent to her two children. She was a white woman, her husband black. She found that it was a nice option to assist her children in understanding some of their ethnic background and the truth about the world. She didn't believe they would get that at school; I believed her.

After another year and a half of struggling with my son in school with his teacher (no real academic issues, mostly behavioral), I decided that the teachers were impeding his ability to learn the information they were teaching in a way that he could be himself. His hyperactivity was a problem for them, so I just decided it was time to try a different way. We began homeschooling the next week.

At the time, I got a lot of people indirectly telling me that it was a bad idea. My father was probably the most vocal because he was "old school" and didn't see this as necessary. He talked about how he too went through the same things with us (his kids), but we turned out fine. He would pick at things Ky wouldn't be able to do without a "formal education." As time went on, the shock of it wore down, and the voices became quiet.

Some of the challenges faced were trying to fill in the now "available homeschool time" with school-related work. Ky is actually quite a bright child and was able to complete his work in a timely manner. Once done, he would ask to play video games or go on the computer. I would say yes, considering he did what he was required for the day. However, I took notice that he would also rush through work or not get some pages done. I didn't notice right away, but too much time was spent not doing any work. Some people said not to worry and to take a more natural approach (especially since his reading is phenomenal, and he wasn't at any disadvantages). However, it bothered me and still does. Not because he isn't doing fine, but because I feel like a complete failure for not filling in that time with more "things" that would require more of my focus. I am self-employed, and my business has been picking up. Plus, we have a baby. All of these things just take a lot of time. That said, we are getting through and seem to be fine because the benefits have been far greater than not.

Ky has expanded his vocabulary and is reading/writing bigger words. His math is good, and he is happier, which is the biggest thing for me. I find that he used to come home with "kiddies depression." Just kid blues from the school day of feeling very boxed in. Now he has so much room to be himself and not feel under a microscope! I can tell that it has allowed him the freedom he needed to be happy. Other than missing his school friends, he seems to enjoy homeschooling.

I haven't experienced anything directly as a black homeschool parent, although there are only a few black families in our homeschool network. Although most of the kids he plays with regularly are black (five of them play hockey with him, and there were another two kids he knew from football), those children are either adopted by white parents or are biracial. I find that the dynamic drives a bit of a wedge in between me really wanting to be friends with them. Not because they are bad people—rather, that eventually something will be said, and they won't react properly. As for the "sista" with the two biracial kids, she seems like she doesn't engage much in the community. Therefore I don't bother in order to avoid the possible "all lives matter" rhetoric. As for the children and their interacting, we have had no problems, and it could remain that way for now. Ky has limited time with them, and I hope that if his time increases, we don't see a negative change.

I would tell anyone who is black and looking to homeschool to go for it! You really have nothing to lose and the world to gain by leading your children's education and allowing them an opportunity to learn according to what is best for them. You can also introduce things and have discussions with them about Afrocentric things and not have to worry that they won't be told the truth at school. The challenges are there, but the rewards are far better. I wouldn't change it for the world!

DORESA'S STORY

I had heard about homeschooling before I even had kids but didn't know much about it. Once I got pregnant with my first, I started reading quite a few books on education and read *The Underground History of*

American Education, by John Taylor Gatto. After that, my husband and I realized public school was probably not going to be the way to go for our kids.

Homeschooling had always been an option for us. We didn't officially decide to homeschool until my eldest did his first year in kindergarten. He was in a private school, and we found even there, they couldn't meet his needs. He was officially diagnosed as being profoundly gifted and severely dyslexic. That combination is hard for any classroom teacher who also has to balance the needs of other children. My twins, who are two years younger, also ended up with the same diagnosis, so it was better all around for all three to be homeschooled.

The most challenging part has honestly been socialization—not for them, for me! While I am mostly an introvert, I do like spending time with close friends. I spend so much time now ensuring my kids get the social experiences they need that I find myself lacking in that area. When I worked full time outside the home, the vast majority of my friends were "work friends." We would chat at the office and do lunch together. When my professional setting changed from in the office to online, there went a lot of my social life! My husband has been great, and I have managed to find one local friend who is also a homeschooler, but things definitely changed for me.

The most rewarding thing is just getting a chance to watch with my own eyes the growth of my children. Now that they are older, I see their true personalities really shine through, and it is very exciting. They are getting opportunities that they could have never gotten in other ways.

I think the biggest stereotype we have had to battle is the idea that all homeschoolers are religious or homeschool for religious reasons. We are secular homeschoolers and aren't trying to provide religious indoctrination of our children. As a result, we don't use traditional homeschooling materials, especially in areas like science and history. Our kids also spend a lot of their social and extracurricular time with children who aren't homeschooled, so they have a very diverse experience that surprises a lot of people.

I would say the biggest negative experience I have faced is that we had not really been openly and aggressively discriminated against until we started homeschooling. My kids went from a diverse and inclusive preschool/kindergarten to my daughter being told by a group of homeschooled preschoolers that "they didn't play with brown kids." Unfortunately, that hasn't changed much. I found that I had to lead or co-lead groups myself because whenever we went to join established general homeschooling groups in our area, the racial tension was unpalatable, and we were openly made to feel uncomfortable. As a lead or co-lead, I find the only people willing to join the groups are those that are more open minded to being around people of color.

I think my biggest advice to aspiring black homeschoolers is to not get too caught up with the "pretty" things you see on social media. People love to post their good days, and some exaggerate how well things go. The first year of homeschooling is the hardest, just like the first year of parenting is the hardest. But, if you focus on bonding and relationship, that makes the rest of the years a lot smoother. I have found that to be the case for us and other more "veteran" homeschoolers that I know.

Know that homeschooling is going to be hard, but it is hard for everyone. However, if you put in the hard work, you will reap the results!

SOME CALL IT THE PUBLIC FOOL SYSTEM

In his ground-breaking book, *Dumbing Us Down: The Hidden Curriculum of Compulsory Education*, John Taylor Gatto shares his experiences as a former public schoolteacher. Gatto taught in New York public schools and was named New York City Teacher of the Year three times and New York State Teacher of the Year in 1991. He worked tirelessly and passionately for the public school system for thirty years, and then he quit. Why? Because he said he no longer wanted to "hurt kids to make a living."[29] One must stop and ask what sort of education Gatto was giving children that would allow him to win teaching awards while simultaneously hurting kids. Well, he answered that question in great detail in his speech "The Seven Lesson School Teacher." He states the following:

> Teaching means different things in different places, but seven lessons are universally taught from Harlem to Hollywood Hills. They constitute a national curriculum you pay for in more ways than you can imagine, so you might as well know what it is…
>
> The first lesson I teach is confusion. Everything I teach is out of context. I teach the un-relating of everything. I teach dis-connections…even in the best schools a close examination of curriculum and its sequence turns up a lack of coherence, full of internal contradictions. Fortunately the children have no words to define the panic and anger they feel at constant violations of natural order. The logic of the school mind is that it is better

to leave school with a tool kit of superficial jargon derived from economics, sociology, natural science and so on, than with one genuine enthusiasm. Think of the great natural sequences—learning to walk and learning to talk; the progression of sunrise to sunset; the ancient procedures of a farmer—all of the parts are in perfect harmony with each other, each action justifies itself and illuminates the past and the future...

The second lesson I teach is class position. My job is to make them like being locked together with children who bear numbers like their own. Or at least to endure it like good sports. If I do my job well, the kids can't even imagine themselves somewhere else, because I've shown them how to envy and fear the better classes and how to have contempt for the dumb classes...

The third lesson I teach is indifference...how I do this is very subtle. I plan lessons very carefully in order to produce this show of enthusiasm. But when the bell rings, I insist they drop whatever it is we have been doing and then proceed to the next work station. They must turn on and off like a light switch...students never have a complete experience except on the installment plan.

The fourth lesson I teach is emotional dependency. By stars and red checks, smiles and frowns, prizes, honors and disgraces I teach you to surrender your will to the predestined chain of command. Rights may be granted or withheld by any authority, without appeal because rights do not exist inside a school, not even the right of free speech, the Supreme Court has so ruled, unless school authorities say they do...

The fifth lesson I teach is intellectual dependency. Good people wait for a teacher to tell them what to do. It is the most important lesson, that we must wait for other people, better trained than ourselves, to make the meanings of our lives. Bad kids fight this, of course, even though they lack the concepts to know what they are fighting, struggling to make decisions for themselves about what they will learn and when they will learn it. How can we allow that and survive as schoolteachers? Fortunately there are procedures to break the will of those who resist...

The sixth lesson I teach is provisional self-esteem... My kids are constantly evaluated and judged. A monthly report, impressive in its precision, is sent into students' homes to signal approval or to mark exactly down to a single percentage point how dissatisfied with their children parents should be.

The seventh lesson I teach is that you can't hide. I teach children they are always watched by keeping each student under constant surveillance as do my colleagues. There are no private spaces for children, there is no private time. Of course I encourage parents to file their own child's waywardness, too... I assign a type of extended schooling called "homework," too, so that the surveillance travels into private households, where students might otherwise use free time to learn something unauthorized from a father or mother, or by apprenticing to some wise person in the neighborhood...Children will follow a private drummer if you can't get them into a uniformed marching band.[30]

If those words do not make your hairs stand on end, I don't know what will. As you can see, the hidden curriculum Gatto speaks of hurts children subtly and psychologically, but it is a double whammy for students of color. Minoritized students must learn to follow an *overt* curriculum that makes them second-guess their self-worth and battle a *covert* curriculum designed to make them feel inferior and untrustworthy. It becomes easy to see why so many "discipline" issues exist within the school system. These are merely teacher-student power struggles. The kids are attempting to voice their grievances within a system that doesn't have the capability to hear them out, the resources to meet their needs, or the time to listen.

I believe it's time to reevaluate charter schools and really investigate the cost/benefit analysis of allowing these schools to become staples in urban communities. Frequent suspensions lead children down a negative path toward school dropout or even prison. These prisons are often owned by the very same entities that used their corporate nonprofit foundations to open charter schools and reap the financial benefits of taxpayer dollars. Charter schools are *helping* the preschool-to-prison pipeline, not working to end it. They do not deserve the blind trust being given to them by people of color.

VOICES OF HOMESCHOOLING PARENTS

FRANK'S STORY

I was curious about homeschooling for quite a while before actually considering it as an option for my family. I was first introduced to the concept as a preteen. A new family moved into our neighborhood and had school-aged children. We often saw them out and about shopping or doing other things with their parents, but never at school! I had a pretty vivid imagination, and so I concocted all sorts of stories for why they weren't at school. Finally, one day the opportunity presented itself. By "presented itself" I mean I couldn't take the curiosity any longer and knocked on their door. That led to a friendship that later answered my questions about homeschooling.

I think the decision to homeschool was one that had been formulating in the back of my mind since my teenage years. I had, and still do have, a *huge* amount of respect for Malcolm X when I first heard his now-famous quote regarding education in the United States: "Only a fool would allow his enemy to educate his children."

I was forced to reconcile that. What were my alternatives? Private school? Relocation? I had exactly *zero* answers, but I definitely had questions! Ultimately the decision came down to an encounter I had with my then eight-year-old's teacher. It was February, and as is customary...time for a "Black History Month report." My daughter loves Marcus Garvey and was excited to write about his work. Her teacher told her "Marcus Garvey isn't on the list" and that she'd have to choose someone else. By my estimation, *any* black history list that doesn't include Garvey is invalid. This school is a charter school, with a 98 percent black staff and probably a 99 percent black student body! I went to the school for more information and was given the list...

Kanye West, Jay-Z, Rihanna, and *Drake* were on the list! I almost couldn't believe what I was reading, so I scheduled a meeting with the principal. I was promptly pushed off on the vice principal, who told me I was "overreacting." I knew in that very second that I was done with public school miseducation.

The most challenging part of homeschooling so far has been realizing that a school day is higher on the priority list than *anything* else. As a business owner and entrepreneur, time is a most valuable asset. Shuffling my work days to be secondary to teaching my children was incredibly difficult and has been a sacrifice!

The most rewarding part of homeschooling has been seeing the connection our girls make with the material. There is truly something magical happening when you see them "get it." There's little else that compares to that feeling. Furthermore, knowing that I'm directly responsible for helping them navigate their education process gives me a sense of security because each day, our bond is reforged!

My personal circle is pretty heavily curated. So much so that the few families we interact with on a personal level fall into one of two categories:

1. They homeschool also.
2. They know me well enough to know that I don't dabble in foolery enough to entertain stereotypes. They know that I'd happily answer *any* genuine questions I could.

There have been a few situations where my daughters and I were out and about after our school day ended, but while tradition school was still in session, where I was asked by perfect strangers (I think as attempts at small talk) about why my daughters were missing school. One time, after an explanation, a curious stranger asked why I decided to homeschool. When I answered (see number 2), I got the most extreme "go to hell" look imaginable. I laughed and counted it as a victory!

I'd tell any would be homeschool parents that it's not as difficult as some might think...and it's not as easy as others might think. Being organized to the nth degree is invaluable, as is patience. Approach homeschooling with the knowledge that you've made one of the most important decisions you could have ever made regarding the upbringing of your child(ren).

Have an easy-to-follow lesson plan that you are familiar with and confident in. Don't be afraid to say "I don't know" if something comes up that you haven't mastered. Roll your sleeves up, get focused, and find the answer together!

Frank is the author of the Jupiter Strong children's book series. You can learn more about his work and purchase a book at jupiterstrong.com.

PRESCHOOL TO PRISON

We've discussed how traditional public schools and charter schools unfairly discipline and alienate children of color in the classroom. Now let's discuss what sort of future lies ahead for "chronic misbehavers" who are pushed out of school and onto the streets.

The first thought that comes to mind is that they are "lost to the system," meaning they no longer have the ability to contribute and help better society. That's good news for corporations in need of cheap labor without the risk of being affiliated with sweatshops. Ranging from as little as ninety cents a day to whopping four dollars a day, prison inmates can act as butchers for McDonald's and Wendy's, make jeans for J. C. Penny, process food for

Aramark Food Services, handle customer service calls for Sprint and AT&T, clean up toxic oil spills, and manufacture uniforms for the US military.[31] Here's the icing on the cake—Walmart utilizes prison labor for everything from cleaning UPC barcodes on products to farming produce. *Yes, the very same company that pumps millions of dollars into low-income, urban charter schools can still cash in on school dropouts.* For the corporate titans at Walmart, it is a win-win whether your children get an education or not. Think about that.

The bright-eyed, innovative, and academically promising students who have their internal fire for education extinguished and tragically end up in prison ironically have something to look forward to. Modern prisons, many of which are owned by both corporate and nonprofit organizations, like the Prisons Foundation, have begun to partner with community colleges to offer higher education to their inmates.

Prisons report collaborating with community colleges for education services because of their low cost, convenient locations throughout the state, status as an accredited post-secondary institution, and willingness to partner. Cost-effective community college fees are more affordable for prisons because: (1) tuition costs and fees at community colleges average $2,272 annually, which is less than half of the annual cost at public four-year institutions ($5,836). Partnerships between prisons and community colleges can lead to significant benefits for all involved—community colleges, prisons, inmates, and the general public. While the mission of community colleges may be the initial incentive for colleges to collaborate with prisons, the additional student population and revenue generated through correctional education further strengthens their commitment to the partnership.[32]

What happens to those artistic students who drop out of school and end up in prison? Well, they can look forward to having their artwork, poems, books, and music lyrics published by the nonprofit the Prison Foundation, which also manufactures erotic art torsos (sex dolls) to help with fundraising. Let's be clear: this is not about bashing correctional facilities and their partner organizations for creating programs that seek to help prisoners challenge themselves academically or express their creativity. Rather, I would like us to question why prisons are becoming work-study programs with cheap corporate labor and day camps for America's marginalized population. All of these prisoners were once students in the inner city or minority neighborhoods who never got the chance to realize their full potential. The 86 percent of black and brown inmates found in prison cells were once children and teens with very few options for success in their communities who were arrested for nonviolent crimes and subsequently became another number in a statistic.

These were students that had the unfortunate fate of attending public schools that spent more time treating them as delinquents instead of as creative human beings. These are kids who only needed a second chance at a better education in a loving environment. If it takes a village to raise a child, then we can certainly say that these were *our* babies being yanked from *our* families. These were our cousins, brothers, fathers, sons, and uncles. These were our sisters, aunts, mothers, and daughters. These were the parents and loved ones who were supposed to help raise the future generation, but instead we now have both parent and child in prison cells.

Why weren't there foundations donating millions of dollars toward recreational facilities, afterschool programs, urban-farming initiatives, job opportunities, and adult learning centers? Where was the *community* approach to bettering the lives of these children—*our* children? Why aren't the prisons full of white children who racked up a series of misdemeanor charges and found themselves incarcerated? I'll tell you why. It's because such an atrocity would never be allowed in the white community. Children raised to be white are raised with a sense of security. White culture is the dominant culture in this nation, and dominance will not yield its power to the livelihood of the peasantry. Please understand that black and brown people are indeed the peasants of this country.

VOICES OF HOMESCHOOLING PARENTS

DANELLE'S STORY

I learned about homeschooling because I am a teacher and try to stay aware of all things "educational." I first explored it for myself when my son Miles was two years old. Before that, when he was a toddler (thirteen months), we knew there was something different about him. He was singing to himself one day, and I realized he was singing the alphabet—phonetically. It wasn't something he'd seen or that I had taught him. From then on, as we paid attention, we realized he could do many things without having been taught. He started reading words before three and was reading chapter books by four. We tried, in vain, to get him into kindergarten early, but the school district wouldn't meet with us. I found out later though that school districts do not get funding for allowing early admissions, so most won't do it. I had also student taught in our homeschool district. The conversations being had by the teachers there—outwardly racist—were the main reason our children wouldn't attend those schools. So we put Miles into a gifted private school for kindergarten and first grades. Kindergarten was great. The teacher was lovely, and he thrived in his learning. The first-grade teacher was just "off" somehow, and I could never put my finger on it, but she just didn't like my kid. As the only nonmodel minority student of color in his class, we wondered if it was a race issue. We also felt she undervalued and underestimated what our child could do. We didn't feel the money we paid equaled the substandard experience he had in school. We decided to pull him out of that school.

We got him into a local environmental-focus magnet school. He loves being outside *and* they let him skip second grade. Win-win, right? Nope. He was still bored in third grade, waiting for every other kid to finish. Nothing new learned. In a class of twenty-four, he was just a well-behaved, quiet kid. We have always done more "school" at home. We continued to do this—supplementing his paltry education until fourth grade. He had started to cry about going to school—hated it really. I went in for visits and realized why. She catered to the lowest-performing students in the class. She made them read *Little House on the Prairie* and learn about Christopher Columbus, and when my kid asked why they learned only about the "bad guys," she asked, "Why does it matter?" Meetings didn't work—so we pulled him out. We let him unschool for a little over a month. This was *hard* for me (as a teacher *and* a mom). But I knew he *needed* it. He read and did some things he was interested in, but for the most part, he did *nothing*. I was exploring other school options. I was a teacher in an urban charter school, and my students also really need a quality education, and I didn't want to be another person who walked out on them midyear. So I brought Miles to school with me some days; he went to my in-laws on the others.

Right now, I am making plans to *not* come back to teaching next year. This is a tough decision. I love teaching. I love having my own money, as a woman, and feeling independent. My professional, hardworking self will struggle with it and miss it. However, as a mother...I know I need to do what is best for my boys (Matias is almost five now). This is a challenge for me personally—this balance.

Homeschooling after school is beyond exhausting. That has been my challenge for these years. How do I not burn out—and how do I keep my boys from also burning out? I am confident this will change when we are together all day next year.

I have heard from some people that my boys need to be "socialized." They aren't wild animals, and being with me all day is socializing. It's a bonus that we are also introverts and don't really get much from being around groups—or being in large classes. I usually just ignore people.

Wanting my sons to have an authentic and true education is very much tied to race. My husband and I grew up getting a "white truth" education—and that's what our children get too. As a teacher, it frustrates us that other teachers don't want to know and do better than what was done for us. It makes me angry that my son has to bring books to school and share them because they library is all white—even on the "black holidays." I don't want him only learning about Martin Luther King Jr., as amazing a human as he was, because he wasn't the only black person to do something amazing. I also want my son to have access to the kind of education that is going to prepare him for his future. I know he is not getting that now.

My advice [to new homeschoolers] would be to start slow, make contacts with people in homeschooling groups that align with your goals and beliefs, and get started. You don't have to be a teacher to teach your child. There are plenty of online and library resources to help you.

KIMBERLEE'S STORY

Our homeschool story is not typical. My husband and I are both products of public education. I even taught school for a few years prior to us becoming a homeschooling family. We sincerely thought that our girls could get a quality education if we simply did our part as parents—researched the schools, moved into the right neighborhood, joined the PTA, and remained involved. The general stuff that you hear you're supposed to do while striving to be a good parent. We were even willing to believe that if we applied to the right magnet programs or charter school, our daughters would get an adequate education. We were wrong. It did not take us several years to realize this; however, it took a while for us to fully digest that so called "good public schools" did not seem to be the same for us as they were for our white parenting peers. Our oldest daughter was just beginning the seventh grade when we removed her from the public schools. Our younger girls were in first grade and kindergarten.

We could see the writing on the wall as soon as our oldest daughter entered the kindergarten. We were encouraged to have her evaluated to see if she had ADHD, only to find out that she is gifted and profoundly so. We had moved from Charlotte, North Carolina, to the Gulf Coast of Alabama. My husband had a job opportunity and thought returning to his home state would serve us well after he had been laid off during the Great Recession.

When my daughter arrived to her new school, she was so full of promise. She tested into the school district's gifted-education program, she was a finalist in the school spelling bee for a couple of years, and she seemed to be thriving academically. Much to our dismay, she had become the target of a neighborhood bully at the bus stop in the mornings. Unbeknown to us, the bully was tormenting our daughter every morning because she was the first to arrive at the bus stop. Eventually the situation spiraled so far out of control that the bully threatened to kill my daughter "with his brother's gun and feed her like jerky" to his dog. At some point his sister got involved in the name-calling, and the school's assistant principal was made aware of the situation by my daughter. The assistant principal even threatened to involve the local police, but never did it dawn on her that she should contact the parents. It wasn't until the bully's parents knocked on our door that we were made aware of the situation.

My husband and I were livid! How on earth could this happen and we not know? I spent countless hours volunteering at the school making copies for teachers, attending PTA meetings, watching classes during lunch—and no one thought to tell me that my daughter was being bullied at school...sigh. We wrote the principal and eventually the superintendent demanding that something be done to make our daughter feel whole again. She was merely a shadow of her old self, and I could see her slipping away from us. The happy look in her eyes was leaving, and I wanted to save her. A true solution and justice never came. We ended up moving to Pittsburgh to what we thought would be greener pastures. My husband had received a promising job opportunity, and we were quite excited about the prospect of living in the Pittsburgh area. We thought the Rust Belt town would rid us of the provincial nature of Southern life.

After having lived in the exurban town of Mars, Pennsylvania, for a year, it became abundantly clear that once one exits the city limits of Pittsburgh, one goes back in time about fifty years. We had seen just as many Confederate flags as we had seen in southern Alabama. There was nothing cosmopolitan about Mars!

During my daughter's first few weeks of school in Mars, I expected to hear from the school's gifted program coordinator regarding her gifted individualized education plan. After nearly a month of no communication, I decided to reach out to the coordinator myself. She was not aware that my daughter had been in a gifted program at her prior school, despite my having all of records sent prior to her arrival and my meeting with the school administration to discuss the gifted program status. Nevertheless, she was retested (this was an extra step created for our daughter—typically testing records from previous schools are used), and gifted identification was not assigned to her until the following school year.

Fast-forward a year, and it had become abundantly clear that we could not continue to put our daughters in such an emotionally unhealthy situation. Our youngest daughter was now entering kindergarten, and I had become an ambassador for a diversity awareness program in the school district. I was on a first-name basis with the superintendent, I volunteered, and I was active in the PTA. I was in and out of their schools every day. Yet we were still very disenchanted with our daughters' academic and social experiences.

Then came the proverbial straw that broke the camel's back. Our then first-grade daughter brought home a book with an insulting racial slur in it. Yes, in 2013! I was in the kitchen preparing a snack for my girls after school, while my daughter was reading the book aloud as part of her nightly homework.

The students were asked to select a book from the teacher's classroom library daily. For reading homework, they were to read the book aloud to their parents, and the parents are to sign a little slip of paper indicating that the book was read. My husband and I had already been in conference with the teacher regarding the lack of challenging curriculum across the subject areas. Our daughter could read at a fourth-grade level at the end of kindergarten and was made to prove that she could all over again at the start of first grade. We felt that she was singled out because of her race. Our daughter was always being told how well-behaved and "good" she was; however, she was not being challenged at all in this environment. The white children in her classroom who were reading at her level seemed to receiving a different level of instruction.

We met with the teacher to demand that our daughter be given equity in her educational plan. The teacher was very condescending to us, and it was clear that she did not want to work in partnership with us. In the end, she agreed to send more challenging books. She also downplayed the district's gifted education plan as an option to provide a challenge to our daughter and stated that "the gifted program is not really that rigorous." So it was quite disturbing when I heard my daughter read aloud the word "Blacky." I stopped preparing dinner and grabbed the book from her, shocked at what I had heard, and quickly scanned the text. I was livid! Not only was the book racially offensive, but it was archaic—printed in 1956 archaic. The book had no business in a teacher's classroom library. We spoke with both the principal and the teacher, and we were told to "watch what comes home." That was their solution. No apology...no "we will comb the shelves to ensure that we have literature that is not racially offensive but is modern and diverse." At that point we knew that we could no longer have our children in a school district that refused to acknowledge their humanity. We began to make plans to homeschool them.

Homeschooling has been a very gratifying for our family. There have been challenges as well. When we first began homeschooling, we did so rather abruptly. We did not have time to plan out our curriculum and procure all of the things that we thought we would need right away, so we enrolled the girls in an online program. Though the online school was light-years better and gave us some autonomy in what was being taught, the girls were connected to a laptop for six hours a day completing assignments and logging in to virtual classrooms. That amount of screen time coupled with the issue of teachers not acknowledging my girls when they wanted to participate in the virtual classroom discussions led us to discontinue the online schooling after a few months. We were quite frankly tired of teachers not seeing our kids academically and meeting them where they are.

We were able to research curriculum and deschool the girls in a few months. Our priority was to really work on repairing their damaged self-esteem. We had to rebuild their curiosity and really work on interpersonal skills initially. There was so much damage done, and, to be honest, we are still uncovering the wounds. I find the flexibility and ability to integrate the girls' passions into our homeschool very rewarding. But nothing is more important to us than providing them with an emotionally safe space to grow and develop. We've found ways to use our library system to enhance their learning, and we invest in museum memberships. We have had some exciting field trips related to our learning, which make the experience authentic for them. When my husband has business trips, we tag along. I would definitely say that our family has become stronger because of homeschooling. My husband teaches the girls music and math occasionally, and he is able to have a more active role in our homeschool than he could have ever had when the girls were attending a traditional school.

We have not experienced much negativity for being homeschoolers. Most people applaud us for being homeschoolers and seem curious about what we are doing. There have been a few times where people seem to be shocked that the girls are homeschoolers because they seemed so "sociable."

However, no stranger has done or said anything to me that was offensive. There can be some competition among homeschooling moms. I typically have a radar for that sort of messiness and avoid those super-competitive types. For that reason, we do our own thing. I have tried the co-op life, and unfortunately that just is not for our family. We live in a largely white community in Connecticut, and coming across black families who homeschool is not common. In fact, we have not met any black homeschoolers in our community since we began our homeschooling journey. Thanks to social media, we have met some incredible black homeschooling families all over the globe. I am so thankful for the virtual support that I have received via social media.

My best advice for new black homeschoolers would be to find a curriculum that works for your child. It's so easy to get caught up with what other homeschooling families are doing; however, you have to consider that each child is unique. What works for them might not work for you. I would also remind new homeschooling families to plan and really evaluate curriculum and materials before purchasing them. Buy a sample, to try it out first. This helps you stay within budget and not be so overwhelmed with too many curriculum products. As the years go by, you will learn what your must-haves are for your homeschool.

During our first year, we spent a fair amount on desks and technology so that we could make sure we had a nice foundation moving forward. Now we no longer have to purchase furniture and computers unless we feel the need to upgrade them. Seek social media connections with other homeschoolers who have similar ideologies. I cannot stress this enough. It is so easy to get caught up in your own little bubble. Seek the advice of homeschooling moms with a similar outlook. This way you are bound to have a bountiful resource of information and tacit knowledge at your fingertips. My social media connections have helped guide me to new curriculum and helped me avoid a few disasters, too. And lastly, organize. I am a work in progress in this area, but I have managed to get better with each passing year. Keep good records of what your student(s) have accomplished in your homeschool. Come up with a system to record your student(s) academic records so that when the time comes for other opportunities and college, you have a record of the work your student has completed in your homeschool.

Part 5: The Home Education Alternative

• • •

Homeschool: A Family-Centered Education

● ● ●

Your children are not your children.

They are sons and daughters of Life's longing for itself.

They come through you but not from you.

And though they are with you yet they belong not to you.

You may give them your love but not your thoughts,

For they have their own thoughts.

You may house their bodies but not their souls,

For their souls dwell in the house of tomorrow, which

you cannot visit, not even in your dreams.

You may strive to be like them, but seek not to make them like you.

For life goes not backward nor tarries with yesterday.

You are the bows from which your children

as living arrows are sent forth.

—KAHLIL GIBRAN

HOMESCHOOLING PROVIDES FAMILIES OF COLOR with a much-needed alternative in the form of a *family-centered education*. I call it a family-centered education because it utilizes the family unit as the foundation of all progress and inspiration. A family is just a small representation of the greater community that resides outside the home. If we can cultivate a genuine sense of gratitude, belonging, resilience, and compassion within our homes, then those characteristics will be the driving forces in our interactions with the world at large.

The black and Latino communities have a long history of placing the family bond and traditions at the center of life's journey and one's own sense of self. There is a strong sense of collective effort and well-being in the power of family to change lives and know the value of extended family within a community. However, our cultural need for community and a sense of purpose has been derailed by the overwhelming demands of the workplace and traditional schooling. These two systems collaborate to create a strained home life that families must battle with on a daily basis. After a hard day's work with coworkers and staff, parents end up spending less time parenting and instead act as chauffeurs, homework managers, referees, and safety monitors. The weekends are supposed to be reserved for actual family time, but even that can often take a backseat to cleaning and running errands. What you end up with is a house full of guarded, agitated, and exhausted individuals who seek solace with their computers, cell phones, and televisions. It takes lot of genuine effort to maintain a strong family bond while balancing the pressures of work and school. The families that thrive under these circumstances should always be applauded.

There is a distinct difference between the *networks* of school and work, which are composed of peer groups and authority figures, and the greater *community*, which is composed of families and neighbors. Networks give us the ability to contribute to society using our mental and physical abilities to achieve a certain goal. Additionally, because networks are built from active effort, they only allow us to share the side of ourselves that comes from a place of executive skill and managerial mindsets. We are not allowed to carry our whole beings into the workplace. The same is true for the traditional school in that it is an institution used to teach children to follow the instruction of authority and share tasks with their peers while appearing enthusiastic about meeting new goals. In both environments, we are always keenly aware that we are being watched, judged, and observed according to our level of productivity, and we respond accordingly. We know that exposing our vulner-abilities can lead to ridicule and punishment, so we wear carefully constructed masks in order to protect ourselves.

In contrast, communities insist that we show up with our whole selves and expose our strengths and weaknesses in effort to find commonalities and build trust. Communities allow us to let our guards down and beckon us to be real, knowing that we will be loved in spite of our flaws because our flaws make us human. We may scream, cry, shout, laugh, sing, and dance. We can discuss our fears and daydream about our futures. We can volunteer our time with those truly in need of our love and care. We can build friend-ships, gain extended family, and create unity. It is in our communities that we feel relaxed, appreciated, and fulfilled. We struggle together, and we grow together.

Homeschooling shows parents on a daily basis that our educational goals and sense of community do not have to be at odds. We can guide our children to academic excellence while valuing them as whole beings. We can watch their eyes light up as they learn something new and take a family road trip while reading aloud. We can volunteer while learning about the value of civic engagement. We can have a cookout and teach the value of kitchen safety. We can learn ancient history while studying art. We can visit a beach and build sand castles while studying architecture. We can play basketball while learn-ing geometry. We can go hiking while studying nature and life science. We can enjoy the wonders of life and grow intellectually. Homeschooling creates freedom, embraces family, and connects communities. Homeschooling uses the village to raise the children.

VOICES OF HOMSCHOOLING PARENTS

NINAH'S STORY

I learned about homeschooling in a most unconventional way. My children and I had the unfortunate experience of being thrust into an unexpected custody battle. I shared a portion of this stressful event with a teacher at my children's school. This teacher told me I would be great at homeschooling my children. She helped me research the laws and find affordable curricula choices available in my state. I was surprised that it was legal to homeschool in all fifty states and that it wasn't a well-known option to most parents. It was a liberating feeling to know that not only did I have a choice in what my children were learning, but that homeschooling support groups were available in my area, as well.

I wasn't sure about homeschooling when we began our homeschooling journey. I homeschooled on a trial basis for a few months. After winning the custody case, I placed my children back in school. After a month of their re-enrollment, I was asked to visit with a few of my children's teachers. I learned that my children were academically ahead of their peers, and their well-mannered behavior stood out! This particular school went through several principals and administration changes during our trial homeschooling year. A new, controversial state test showed most of the children in our district were academically behind students in neighboring districts. I transferred my children to a charter school and quickly learned the school was state run, as well. The charter school was so focused on academic results that it ignored the individuality of the students. A teacher whom I admired told me it would be an investment in my children to continue to homeschool them. I quite literally ran with that advice and haven't looked back!

The most challenging part of homeschooling was believing in myself—learning that although I am my children's first teacher, I am not their only teacher. It was slightly challenging to accept that I didn't have a village to support us and that I had to go out and build one. Once I learned that there were thousands of curricula choices, I felt overwhelmed. The more I researched, while allowing my children to get used to not responding to a bell and constant commands, I realized by watching them play, choosing curriculum tailored to their learning style was easy!

I homeschooled while married to an abusive man and through a very tough divorce. I was the only parent allowed to homeschool while living in a domestic violence shelter. I worked two jobs and built a business while homeschooling. Sometimes we schooled at night, sometimes not at all. I homeschooled through homelessness, living briefly on Section 8 and unemployment benefits, through relocating to another state. The challenge was to never stop, no matter what my circumstances were. I chose to teach my children that there are no obstacles too big to keep you from reaching your goals. They don't have to read about motivation and defeating all odds in a book; they've lived through those character-building moments with me.

One of the most rewarding discoveries in schooling my children at home is that they teach me as I teach them! We all learn together. We understand one another's learning styles and can now point out one another's growth. I love hearing strangers compliment my children's intelligence and great communication skills with people of all ages and note their acts of kindness.

I have had strangers enjoy my children's company until they found out they were homeschooled. We have been berated in more than one grocery store, science fair, and museum about my lack of credentials to teach my own children at home. We've been turned away from "inclusive" homeschooling groups because we are not religious. My children have learned not to defend my choice but to lead by example. While these experiences are becoming rare occurrences for us, my children know that there are people who are afraid to think outside of the box. This teaches them to consider the opinions of people who think differently than they do and choose the manner in which they respond. Stereotypes are very limiting. We choose to break them down and show the world how we roll!

I have had family members tell me that I was going to ruin my children. I have had a white teacher tell me I wasn't good enough to give my children a world-class education while handing my child a scholarship for excelling in his class. My mother used to think I was schooling my children "wrong." I allowed her to use her method—the traditional brick-and-mortar method at home—for a day. It was hilarious to watch her exert authority over their every move. My children asked her many questions and wanted her to show them "her work." After watching her become more frustrated by the minute, I stepped in and asked her to listen to her "students." By the end of the "school day," she admitted that homeschooling three children was harder than it looked—if you didn't listen and learn with them.

It's not enough to love your children. You have to like them, too! Be willing to be open to the way they learn. Be open to learning what you thought you knew from a different perspective. My youngest child thrives on the high-functioning autism spectrum. Being able to see the world from his view has enhanced my education, compassion, and empathy. Utilize your local resources. Parks, museums, nature trails, grocery stores: every place you visit is a place of learning. Learning to enjoy the very presence of your children is more important than using the latest, greatest curricula. Your children will learn. Build a village of mentors, teachers, and people who support your vision for your children. When you find yourself on the brink of giving up, remember the reason you chose to embark on this challenging yet very rewarding journey. Don't forget to include your children regarding your vision. Being able to teach your children from a black perspective is a gift that keeps on giving, generation after generation. Never give up—your children are watching you!

Ninah is the creator and founder of Getchu Some Free, a nonprofit organization that assists women in rebuilding their self-esteem and gaining self-love. You can learn more at facebook.com/getchusomefree.

Opting Out and Moving Forward

• • •

I, too, sing America.

I am the darker brother.

They send me to eat in the kitchen

When company comes,

But I laugh,

And eat well,

And grow strong.

Tomorrow, I'll be at the table

When company comes.

Nobody'll dare

Say to me,

"Eat in the kitchen," Then.

Besides,

They'll see how beautiful I am

And be ashamed

—"I, Too, Am America," by Langston Hughes

I DO NOT WRITE OUT of spite. I do not write out of anger. I write out of disappointment and conviction. I write in hope for a better future. I write to give our communities a voice.

We have become exhausted with the current state of affairs and disillusioned by the supposed socioeconomic advancements in this country. Our communities have consistently held hands at the bottom of every statistic relating to social and economic progress, and that is a disheartening but indisputable fact.

It is unfortunate that we do not live in a country that affords equal opportunities to all of its citizens. It is unfortunate that black and Latino parents aren't homeschooling solely out of curiosity and desire but instead out of genuine need.

It is unfortunate that we live in a democratic country that only strives to meet the needs and human rights of a select few, while ignoring the suffering of others. It is unfortunate that the education system is too broken to merit waiting any further for its repair.

The Black and Latino communities have tried in vain for decades to remain patient with the public school system and optimistic with private and charter schools. However, all three institutions have failed to place our children in equal standing with White students as a whole. Our children have suffered emotionally, physically, and mentally while the nation we call home turned a blind eye. It is for this reason that we have opted out and have decided to homeschool.

We unapologetically believe that our children deserve a top-notch education that prepares them for future success and technological innovation. We unapologetically believe that our children should be treated with loving-kindness and protected from bullying and demeaning teachers. We unapologetically believe that our children deserve to be surrounded by educators who see them as whole beings with thoughts, goals, talents, and ambitions. We unapologetically believe that our children should be able to embrace their creativity and enjoy the inherent freedoms of childhood. We unapologetically believe that our children should not be unfairly penalized for their shortcomings or ridiculed for their mistakes. We unapologetically believe that a world-class education is a birthright of all citizens, regardless of income or racial identity.

We do not homeschool because we want to, but rather we homeschool because we have to. We homeschool because our children depend on us. We homeschool because the nation has challenged us all to pave the way toward a brighter future, and we proudly accept that challenge.

Hold fast to dreams
For if dreams die
Life is a broken-winged bird
That cannot fly.
Hold fast to dreams
For when dreams go
Life is a barren field
Frozen with snow.

—Langston Hughes

Q&A Section

● ● ●

"I'M READY TO TAKE THE plunge and homeschool my child. Where do I begin?"

✤ Firstly, I must applaud your decision to embark on the beautiful journey of homeschooling! The rewards are plentiful. Secondly, you can find tons of resources and useful information on my site, empoweredhomeed.com. I created the site to be a one-stop shop for all of the parents I've encountered needing assistance and guidance with the homeschool process. I guarantee you'll love it!

"Are you against public school?"

✤ I am not against the idea of a free public education for all citizens. It is a noble idea to provide such a service to the nation, and I view education as a human right, not a luxury. However, I do not support the public school system as it stands today. The system is terribly flawed and in need of serious repair, and such massive changes take more time than we would like to admit. Therefore, I support homeschooling as an educational solution for action-oriented persons.

"I'm a single parent. How could I possibly homeschool?"

- The answer lies in the value of community. Being a single mother does not mean you have to do everything on your own. Find a home-school community or *build* a homeschool community of like-minded parents where you can share childcare responsibilities with each other (watching each other's kids) and work together on teaching the children. Additionally, with the mobility provided by the Internet, you can get a job working from home with a reputable company that allows you to have control of your work schedule. There are many options available if you open yourself up to it. It takes a village to raise a child, and you can be a part of one!

"How do I make sure my kids have a social life? I don't want them to be weird and isolated."

- Neither do I! Please don't think for a second that homeschooling your children means that they will actually be at home all day. That is not the case! There are so many weekly homeschool outings and monthly educational programs that kids of all ages can attend. Practically every museum, zoo, aquarium, and nature preserve have enrichment programs (many specifically for homeschool families) that allow kids to learn and build friendships. Additionally, there is a plethora of extracurricular activities (sports, dance, chess clubs, etc.) that your kids can be involved in to meet other children who share their interests. It is in these spaces that authentic friendships are made. Relax; they'll be fine.

"How do I make time for myself as a homeschooling parent? Won't I be with my children all day?!"

* Self-care is so very important to our well-being as parents and individuals. I highly recommend incorporating time for yourself as part of the *daily* schedule. And I mean literally carve out hours at the end of the day or early in the morning before the kids wake up to give yourself quiet reflection, reading time, workout time, and so on so that you can be a fully present parent. I also suggest having a day once or twice a month set aside as a full day of relaxation away from the children.

"How can I afford to homeschool? I can't imagine the costs associated with it!"

* You would be pleased to know that you can actually homeschool your child for pennies on the dollar or even free. There are tons of options when it comes to curriculum, and any budget can be accommodated without watering down the educational content. I have several resources readily available on the website empoweredhomeed.com. The site is very user friendly, and you can easily find the best curriculum for your family's needs. We also must admit that even public school isn't truly free—you have to buy school supplies and school clothes, pay for class field trips, pay for lunch, pay for gas needed to commute, and so on. We don't have to break the bank to educate our kids, but we must also see the money spent on our child's education as an investment of the highest caliber.

Part 1

Bibb, Henry. "Narrative of the Life Adventures of Henry Bibb, an American Slave." In *African American Slave Narratives*, edited by Sterling Lecatur Bland Jr., 355. Westport: Greenwood Press, 2001.

Williams, Heather Andrea. *Self-Taught: African American Education in Slavery and Freedom*. Chapel Hill: University of North Carolina Press, 2005.

Goodell, William. *The American Slave Code in Theory and Practice: Its Distinctive Features Shown by Its Statutes, Decisions, and Illustrative Facts*. New York:American and Foreign Anti-Slavery Society, 1853.

Finkelman, Paul, ed. *State Slavery Statutes*. Frederick: University Publications of America, 1989.

Hutchison, A., comp. *Code of Mississippi: Being an Analytical Compilation of the Public and General Statutes of the Territory and State, with Tabular References to the Local and Private Acts, from 1798–1848*. Jackson: 1848.

Walker, Vanessa Siddle. *Their Highest Potential: An African American School Community in the Segregated South*. Chapel Hill: University of North Carolina Press, 1996.

Martha L. Kellog, January 3, 1863, in American Missionary, March 1863, 64-65.

Part 2

Gandara, Patricia C., and Frances Contreras. *The Latino Education Crisis: The Consequences of Failed Social Policies.* Cambridge: Harvard University Press, 2009.

Valenzuela, Angela. *Subtractive Schooling: U.S.-Mexican Youth and the Politics of Caring.* Albany: State University of New York, 1999.

"Latinos in America: A Demographic Overview." *Immigration Policy Center.* American Immigration Council, Apr. 2012. Web. Accessed May 8, 2016.

Goldring, R., L. Gray, and A. Bitterman. "Characteristics of Public and PrivateElementary and Secondary School Teachers in the United States: Results from the 2011–12 Schools and Staffing Survey." (NCES August 2013-314), Contract No. ED-IES-12-D-005, Department of Education. Washington, DC: National Center for Education Statistics. Retrieved May 8, 2016 http://nces.ed.gov/pubsearch.

Rich, Motoko. "Where Are All the Teachers of Color?" Sunday Review News Analysis, *New York Post.* Apr.11, 2015.

LoBuglio, S. "Time to Reframe Politics and Practices in Correctional Education." In *Annual Review of Adult Learning and Literacy, Vol. 2.* Eds. J. Comings, B. Garner, and C. Smith. San Francisco: Jossey-Bass, (February 2, 2010.

Stephan, J. J. "State Prison Expenditures, 1996." Washington, DC: US Department of Justice, Bureau of Justice Statistics. NCJ 172211.

Providing Workforce Education and Training to Reduce Recidivism. Office of Vocational and Adult Education, Partnerships between Community Colleges and Prisons. Washington, DC: US Department of Education, 2009.

Hemlock, Doreen. "'None of the Above' Wins Referendum in Puerto Rico." *Sun Sentinel.* December 14, 1998.

Goldring, R., L. Gray, and A. Bitterman. "Characteristics of Public and Private Elementary and Secondary School Teachers in the United States: Results from the 2011–12 Schools and Staffing Survey." (NCES August 2013-314), Contract No. ED-IES-12-D-005, Department of Education. Washington, DC: National Center for Education Statistics. Retrieved May 8, 2016 http://nces.ed.gov/pubsearch.

"Documentation for the 2011–12 Schools and Staffing Survey." US Department of Education. Washington, DC: National Center for Education Statistics.

Cochran, W. G. *Sampling Techniques.* New York: John Wiley and Sons, 1977.

Stoelinga, Sarah. "Critical Issues in Urban Education." *Coursera.* Feb. 2016. Web. Accessed Aug. 8, 2016.

Part 3

Alexander, Shawn Leigh. *W. E. B Du Bois: An American Intellectual and Activist*. Rowman and Littlefield, Danvers, MA. July 2, 2015.

Mack, Raymond W. "School Desegregation: Case Studies of Conflict and Change." In *Our Children's Burden: Studies of Desegregation in Nine American Communities,*Random House. New York, NY: Vintage Books, 1968.

Wells, Amy Stuart, et al. *Both Sides Now: The Story of School Desegregation's Graduates*. University of California Press, Oakland,CA, 2009.

Part 4

DeRuy, Emily. "How Americans View Vary on Whether Children Have Equal Access to Same Opportunities." *The Atlantic*. Mar. 10, 2016.

———. "In Wealthier Schools, Students Are Further Apart." *The Atlantic*. May 3, 2016.

———. "Unequal Discipline at Charter Schools." *The Atlantic*. Mar. 18, 2016.

———. "White Teachers Expect Less Than Black Teachers from Black Students." *The Atlantic*. Apr. 1, 2016.

Berkshire, Jennifer. "The System Works." EduShyster2012. June 8, 2016. Retrieved May 8, 2016 Edushyster.com

Goldring, R., S. Taie, L. Rizzo, D. Colby, and A. Fraser. *User's Manual for the 2011–12 Schools and Staffing Survey Volumes 1–6.* (NCES 2013-330 through 2013-335). US Department of Education. Washington, DC: National Center for Education Statistics. 2013.

US Department of Education, National Center for Education Statistics. (2003). NCES Statistical Standards (NCES 2003-601). Washington, DC: US Government Printing Office.

Gibran, Khalil. *The Prophet.* Alfred. A. Knopf, New York, NY, 1923.

Gatto, John Taylor. *Dumbing Us Down: The Hidden Curriculum of Compulsory Education.* New Society Press, Gabriola, BC 1992.

US Department of Education, Office of Vocational and Adult Education, Partnerships between Community Colleges and Prisons: Providing Workforce Education and Training to Reduce Recidivism, Washington, DC, 2009.

Kozol, Jonathan. *The Shame of a Nation: The Restoration of Apartheid Schooling in America.* Broadway Paperbacks, New York, NY 2005.

Landsberg, Mitchell. "Spitting in the Eye of Mainstream Education." *Los Angeles Times.* May 31, 2009. Web. Accessed Aug. 10, 2016.

Rich, Motoko. "A Walmart Fortune: Spreading Charter Schools." *New York Times*. Apr. 25, 2014. Web. Accessed Aug. 10, 2016.

Ravitch, Diane. "How Billionaires Are Successfully Fooling Us into Destroying Public Education—and Why Privatization Is a Terrible Idea." AlterNet. Basic Books. July 21, 2016. Accessed Aug. 10, 2016. Alternet.com

Jackson, Abby. "The Walmart Family Is Teaching Hedge Funds How to Profit from Publicly Funded Schools." *Business Insider*. Mar. 17, 2015. Web. Accessed Aug. 10, 2016.

Jackson, Abby. "Here's How Millions of Dollars Flow from Wall Street to Charter Schools." *Business Insider*. Mar. 18, 2015. Web. Accessed Aug. 10, 2016.

Henderson, Alex. "9 Surprising Industries Getting Filthy Rich from Mass Incarceration." Salon.com. AlterNet. Feb. 22, 2015. Web. Accessed Aug. 10, 2016.

"13 Mainstream Corporations Benefiting from the Prison Industrial Complex." *Atlanta Black Star*. Oct. 10, 2014. Web. Accessed Aug. 10, 2016.

Part 5

Delgado, Angelica. "Police Brutality: Impacts on Latino and African American Lives and Communities." 2016. Matt Meier Award. Paper 1. http://scholarcommons.scu.edu/meier_award/1.